Curriculum Development for Legal English Programs

Curriculum Development for Legal English Programs

By

Halina Sierocka

CAMBRIDGE SCHOLARS
PUBLISHING

Curriculum Development for Legal English Programs,
by Halina Sierocka

This book first published 2014

Cambridge Scholars Publishing

12 Back Chapman Street, Newcastle upon Tyne, NE6 2XX, UK

British Library Cataloguing in Publication Data
A catalogue record for this book is available from the British Library

ISBN (10): 1-4438-5437-9, ISBN (13): 978-1-4438-5437-5

CONTENTS

Part II

List of Tables

PREFACE

The „*Curriculum Development for Legal English Program*" endeavours to combine both the theory and practice of English for Specific Purposes in the Legal English context. This book is aimed at helping teachers of Legal English to design their own courses or modify existing ones exploiting their own experiences or the outcomes of research conducted by others.

The book is in two parts. Part I which comprises four chapters relates to the theory of ESP curriculum development in the Legal English context. Chapter One discusses basic concepts in ESP i.e. some attempts are made to define the notion of ESP. In addition, the conditions and process of learning and teaching ESP and the role of the ESP teacher are examined. Special importance is put on the subject-knowledge dilemma and co-operative teaching. Finally, language issues i.e. the proportion of grammar and vocabulary and their roles in ESP teaching/learning along with the specificity of legal discourse are discussed. Chapter Two is devoted to syllabus design for ESP – choosing the most appropriate syllabus type, conducting needs analysis among the target group, selecting and grading syllabus content and finally evaluating the implemented syllabus. Chapter Three describes the types of materials that may be selected for ESP courses. Special emphasis is put on the role of authentic and teacher-generated materials. This chapter also includes models for materials evaluation. Chapter Four presents key issues in assessing and testing languages for specific purposes and describes two leading public examinations in Legal English i.e. the Test of Legal English Skills (TOLES) and the ILEC (the International Legal English Certificate). Part II includes a model syllabus for a course of English for Legal English which is the outcome of a three-year research programme carried out among legal professionals (i.e. law students, academics and lawyers – practitioners) in Poland. Chapter V presents the course description, objectives and content with examples of techniques and teaching resources that can be exploited in any Legal English class.

I would like to thank Professor Hanna Komorowska for her care and guidance in the preparation of this book. Her advice and suggestions have enormously contributed to the outcome of the work. I also wish to thank Dr Barbara Polityńska and Dr Dorota Potocka for their feedback and help in the preparation of this book for publication.

LIST OF ABBREVIATIONS

CEFR	Common European Framework of Reference
CIPP	Context – Input – Process - Product
EAP	English for Academic Purposes
EGAP	English for Academic General Purposes
EGBP	English for Business General Purposes
EOP	English for Occupational Purposes
ESP	English for Special Purposes
ILEC	International Legal English Certificate
LSP	language(s) for specific purposes
PSA	Present Situation Analysis
SSI	subject-specialist informant
SWOT	strengths – weaknesses – opportunities - threats
TBLT	task-based language teaching
TL	target language
TLU	target language use
TSA	Target Situation Analysis
TOLES	Test of Legal English Skills

PART I

CHAPTER ONE

BASIC CONCEPTS IN ENGLISH FOR SPECIFIC PURPOSES (ESP)

1. Defining ESP

The definition of ESP is a highly debated issue. Whilst numerous scholars have endeavoured to define the concept of ESP, others have cast doubt on whether it is at all possible to do so, and still others have reserved their judgment, only to wonder at how special the field really is.

The debate was precipitated by a simple clarification of the term "special" and whether it applied to the language or to the specialized aims of ESP. It was first made by Perren in 1974 and completed by Mackay and Mountford in 1978 (after Gatehouse 2001). They suggested that the word "special" in ESP should be understood as **"special" purpose** for which learners learn and not the "special" language that they learn.

One of the first definitions of ESP was provided by Hutchinson & Waters (1987) who claimed that ESP should be perceived as **an approach** rather than as a product. They explained that **students' needs** are the foundation of ESP, in particular referring to the language required and the learning context. Their needs are understood as the reasons for which students are learning English and as they vary, their learning purposes will be different too.

Strevens (1988), on the other hand, in his definition of ESP makes a distinction between four **absolute characteristics** and two **variable characteristics**. The absolute characteristics were described as:

- designed to meet specified needs of the learner,
- related in content to particular disciplines, occupations and activities,
- centered on language appropriate to those activities in syntax, lexis, discourse, semantics and analysis of the discourse,
- in contrast with General English.

Whereas the variable characteristics meant that ESP:

- may be restricted as to the learning skills to be learned,
- may not be taught according to any pre-ordained methodology.

Robinson (1991) alternatively uses two criteria and a number of characteristics to define ESP. The two criteria are the following:

- ESP is normally goal-directed,
- needs analysis contributes to the development of courses and should specify precisely what students will use English for.

The characteristics involve:

- the limited period of time in which the objectives should be achieved,
- homogenous classes of adults in terms of the work or specialist studies the students are involved in.

Jordan (1997:3-4), on the other hand, endeavours to define the concept of ESP by examining the relationships between study skills and ESP needs. According to Jordan, we learn English for three types of purposes:

1) **General Purposes** – even though they are called General Purposes, students study foreign languages for no particular purpose; although (in their opinion) they have no obvious reason, they study because they have to;
2) **Social Purposes** – students study English for conversational purposes and communicative situations like shopping, telephoning as well as "survival" English.
3) **Special Purposes** – they study English either because they need English at work or at university. This distinction results in two strands of ESP i.e. English for Occupational/Vocational Purposes (EOP) or English for Academic Purposes (EAP) and is further discussed by many researchers such as Jordan (1997:1), Dudley-Evans & St. John (1998:7), Flowerdew & Peacock (2001: 8) Hyland & Hamp-Lyons (2002: 2) who describe English for Academic Purposes as the language of research and instruction relating to the specific communicative needs and practices of particular groups in academic contexts whereas English for Occupational/Vocational Purposes (EOP) "refers to English that is not for academic purposes; it includes professional purposes in administration, medicine, law and business" Dudley-Evans & St. John (1998:7). Nevertheless, as Flowerdew & Peacock (2001: 8) observe, the distinction between EAP and EOP is not precise. A

lot of language learnt at university may be used by students in their prospective professional domains.

The most elaborate definition of ESP is produced by Dudley-Evans & St. John (1998), who modify Streven's original definition of ESP and also refer to the concept of absolute and variable characteristics. These are presented in the chart below.

Absolute characteristics of ESP	**Variable characteristics of ESP**
• ESP is designed to meet the specific needs of the learner, • ESP makes use of the underlying methodology and activities of the disciplines it serves, • ESP is centred on the language, skills, discourse and genres appropriate to these activities.	• ESP may be related to, or designed for, specific disciplines, • ESP may use, in specific teaching situations, a different methodology from that of general English, • ESP is likely to be designed for adult learners, either at a tertiary level institution or a professional work situation, • ESP is generally designed for intermediate or advanced students.

Table 1-1. The concept of absolute and variable characteristics of ESP by Dudley-Evans & St. John (1998)

For opponents of the idea of ESP (often described as a "**wide angle approach"**) – it (ESP) is nothing other than General English for Specific Purposes. They claim that "there are generic skills and forms of language that are the same across a range of disciplines, professions or purposes" (Hutchinson & Waters 1987:165–166, Spack 1988 after Hyland 2002) and there are not sufficient reasons for a subject-specific approach. This view is supported by Widdowson (1998:3-4, 2003) who develops the discussion over the specificity of ESP. He understands it as the specific use of language put in a particular context or situation but not as a specific language or code in itself. He argues that in a pragmatic sense, all uses of English are somehow specific, as they serve particular purposes: people produce both written and oral utterances to achieve certain purposes, taking into consideration the recipient's knowledge and they do that with little effort. Thus he claims that English for Specific Purposes is nothing other than communication in English in general, and states that it is difficult to establish a definition of ESP as such. Finally, Zhang (2007) quotes Nelson's (2000) survey which revealed that the core of ESP is "to identify learner needs and to design ways of meeting these needs instead of conducting a systematic study of English in use in the specific field or activity".

2. Methodology of ESP

The methodology of ESP has been subjected to numerous discussions and debates. The core issue in these considerations is whether or not there is a special methodology of ESP and whether such a methodology is needed.

Hyland (2002) in his article poses the question: "how far should we go now with specificity?" and presents the problem in great detail. He reports that according to some scholars there are insufficient reasons to justify the need for implementing a special methodology for ESP as:

- it is impossible to identify and teach specific varieties of language (Spack 1988 after Hyland), therefore teaching subject content in a foreign language should be left to the subject specialists themselves, as language teachers are not the experts in a particular professional domain and they should concentrate on the general principles of language teaching,
- the subject – matter domain requires a higher level of English proficiency so the learners first need to acquire general English at the appropriate level,
- times of "cut-backs" cannot justify the systematic analyses of tasks and texts.

As a consequence, Hyland (2002:392) remarks, that in practice ESP is often regarded as "as a 'service activity', shunted off into special units, and marginalised as a remedial exercise designed to fix-up students' problems". He also notes that such solutions are more convenient for university administrators, who find them cheaper and logistically easier to implement.

Other scholars argue, however, that the methodology of ELT differs only insignificantly from the methodology of ESP. Robinson (1991), for example, questions the specificity of ESP methodology stating that only two characteristic features of ESP can be identified:

- ESP activities derive from the students' specialism (nevertheless, it is not a *sine qua non* condition),
- ESP activities can (but may not) have an authentic purpose derived from the students' target needs.

Hence, it is difficult to present an explicit and clear statement as to whether or not ESP borrowed ideas from ELT or vice versa.

This view is supported by Watson Todd (2003: 147-156), who claims that the only distinguishing factor between ESP and ELT is team teaching (understood as cooperating with content teachers). The other approaches emphasized in EAP literature i.e. inductive learning, process syllabus, learner autonomy, use of authentic materials and tasks, integration of teaching and technology can also be found in general English language teaching.

Conversely, Dudley-Evans & St. John (1998) emphasize the point that specific ESP teaching has its own methodology, by which they mean that:

- all ESP teaching should reflect the methodology of the disciplines and professions it serves,
- the activities the students need to carry out, generate and depend on registers and genres associated with the language that students need to be able to manipulate in order to carry out the activity,
- the interaction between students and teacher may differ from that which occurs in the general English class.

It is also maintained that in ESP classes generally, the interaction may be similar to that in a General English class; however, in the more specific ESP classes, the teacher sometimes becomes more like a language adviser and consultant, having equal status with the learners, who are often experts in the subject matter.

Also, Hyland (2002) argues the case for specificity, underlining the benefits of specialized methodology for ESP and providing a number of counterarguments for the opponents of this approach:

- the necessity of learning generic language forms and functions by weaker students before they concentrate on ESP is not supported by any research in applied linguistics,
- subject-specialists are not necessarily better teachers of specialized discourse; they do not generally teach literacy skills and find discourse conventions self-evident and universal, therefore in their mind, there is no need to explain or teach them,
- it was the economic aspect that stimulated the development of ESP and it is still a crucial issue in many companies and corporations which actively seek, employ and highly value specialist practitioners in order to increase the cost-effectiveness of the company,
- students do not learn in a

> "vacuum: their disciplinary activities are a central part of their engagement with others in their disciplines and they communicate effectively only by using its particular conventions appropriately."
>
> (Hyland 2002:393)

Finally, Hyland (2002) emphasizes, that thanks to the special methodology, concepts such as genre, authenticity or communicative purpose appear and develop. It may be considered expensive, time-consuming and skill-intensive, but students have an opportunity to develop the skills which allow them to participate in particular academic and professional contexts actively, and which at the same time, makes the teaching more effective.

Many researchers such as Gaffield-Vile (1996), Celani (2003), Dovey (2006), Kim (2006) and Zhang (2007) support Hyland's idea and remark that in order to achieve professional success, students have to have a higher proficiency of academic and vocational English and the discourse of specific disciplines.

2.1 The conditions and process of learning and teaching ESP

Basturkmen (2006:85-86) discusses two conditions needed for language learning and how the ideas are reflected in ESP teaching. These are: **acculturation** and **input and interaction**.

Acculturation is based on the idea that ESP learners need to be close to their target discourse community, "to be socially and psychologically integrated into their target discourse community", which is an indispensable factor for learning the specific –purpose language. As Baskurkmen (2006:88-89) remarks, there are numerous ESP teaching approaches to familiarize learners with the language practices of target discourse communities. She however doubts whether it is enough for students to learn ESP. The issue of acculturation is especially discussed in relation to the genre-based approach. It follows Swales' definition of genres which are to signal the discourse community's norms, ways of thinking and constructing knowledge.

Wharton (as cited in Basturkmen 2006) distinguishes **three models of acculturation** in relation to genre-based approaches in ESP:

- **Induction** – learning about and practice of the genre takes place "in vitro" – the ESP course is held prior to students gaining experience in the target discourse community; the ESP teacher introduces the genre used in the target discourse community alongside their associated cultural aspects; the learners, on the other hand, may practise the genre in the language classroom. The induction model is common in the teaching of ESP; it is however, criticized by some writers. Wharton (1999) claims that students who have some experience of genres in their language, often experience difficulties with acquiring the genre in a second language, due to the fact that they have learnt the ways of thinking and values referring to the original system and the second system may be perceived as contradictory to the original one. It is especially observable in Legal English where there are two diverse systems of laws – continental (based on codes) and common law systems (based on precedents). The differences in the institutions and terms may result in confusion and misunderstanding. The induction model represents a weak form of the acculturation theory – "the learners are observers of the discourse practice and values of inside members" (Basturkmen, 2006:90). This model of teaching takes places mainly at the tertiary level where students are taught ESP in the framework of their curriculum.
- **Adjunct** – the students of ESP courses concurrently participate in the target discourse community and ESP courses. The ESP courses support learners while acquiring genre in target discourse

community situations often providing essential information about the genre they meet during these events.

- **Apprenticeship or mentoring** – ESP is taught to provide learners mainly with linguistic assistance as ESP learners acquire the genre first and foremost in the target discourse community. This model represents the strongest version of the acculturation theory – the student acquires the language and learns how to communicate by being a member of the discourse community whereas the ESP instructor acts as a language instructor. This model of acquiring ESP is common among adult professionals (people who are members of the profession) who are familiar with the genre and want to master their communication skills.

Another theory discussing the conditions needed for language learning in ESP teaching refers to the concept of **input and interaction**. It is based on Krashen's Input Hypothesis (1982) enriched by Long's Interaction Hypothesis (1996) – the main objective is to create the conditions in which successful language learning is believed to occur. The following requisites are mentioned:

- learners acquire the language by understanding messages clear to them,
- learners only learn what they are prepared to learn,
- linguistic input is required,
- learners negotiate the meaning of the input to understand it better,
- negotiated input fits the needs of each learner and becomes intake.

Long (1996) underlines the importance of negative feedback in the process of ESP learning. The negative feedback (for example error correction) contributes to acquisition of ESP providing learners with the information they need to notice the gap between their own production and target language forms.

Five main objectives in teaching ESP provided by Basturkmen (2006:133-146) are:

- revealing subject specific language use,
- developing target performance competences,
- teaching underlying knowledge,
- developing strategic competence,
- fostering critical awareness.

Revealing subject specific language use is the teaching objective which has prevailed in ESP and is aimed both at showing how English is used in the target environment and sharing the knowledge acquired in linguistic research in that area. The objective confirms Bhatia's idea (1982), in which he suggested that teachers should simplify sample texts so that structures used in the genre are clearer to the learners and in that way, the outcomes of linguistic research might be implemented into teaching English to law students.

This approach, however, is criticized by Wharton (1999) who argues that teaching and learning a genre is not just transmission of linguistic information. He argues that:

- learners perceive acquiring professional genre as difficult, since it requires not only "conceptual understanding of the surface discourse but also of a set of socially valued norms and thus new frameworks of reasoning",
- professional genres are frequently mastered late even in the learner's first language,
- teachers tend to be unfamiliar with the nature of a genre thus the communication between a teacher and a learner is intricate.

Developing target performance competences is the teaching objective which emphasizes the role of needs analysis. Needs analysis divulges the demands and expectations of the target environment and teaching ESP is aimed at developing the learners' abilities to perform the activities of the profession and to function to the standards expected in that profession. Munby (1978) with his Communicative Needs Processor, might be considered the forerunner of this approach in teaching ESP oriented towards the demands of the target environment. He claimed that courses could be arranged around communicative events in which ESP learners would be involved in their target environment and the needs analysis would help to identify the communicative events which occur in the target environment.

Basturkmen (2006) claims that using a foreign language for special purposes also requires knowledge and understanding of concepts relating to the professional domain, as well as linguistic proficiency and knowledge; therefore **teaching underlying knowledge** should be a component of ESP courses. The view is supported by Douglas (2000) who claims that specific-purpose language ability results from an interaction between specific background knowledge and language ability. The approach is not new, however. Hutchinson and Waters (1985) introduced the term "*underlying competencies*" by which they meant teaching general conceptual subject content alongside the language.

Douglas (2000) emphasizes that not only language knowledge (grammatical, functional, textual etc.) and background knowledge of the professional domain but also strategic competence constitute specific-purpose language ability, thus **developing strategic competence** is crucial. "As a link between context and language knowledge, strategic competence is assumed to operate in all communicative situations" Douglas (2000: 38).

As Basturkmen (2006) points out, teaching ESP to students who are legal professionals (who have either professional experience or have experience in the study of their disciplines) could be targeted in order to develop students' strategic competence. She argues that:

> " the intent is to bring to the surface the knowledge of the subject area that the students already have and to create opportunities for the students to actualize this knowledge in the target language" Basturkmen (2006:139).

A critical approach to ESP teaching is also present in the literature:

- Widdowson (1983) claims that ESP teaching is more a form of training behaviours rather than language education. In his opinion, unlike general English, ESP does not distinguish aims (understood as the eventual target behaviours of the students) and objectives (perceived as the pedagogical means which enable the students to achieve the behaviours). Thus, ESP courses specify where the learners should end up, rather than working out the pedagogical means to achieve those ends. Moreover, ESP courses tend to endow learners with a restricted set of language competencies (just to function in the target environment) whereas general English provides learners with the strategies which enable them to solve difficulties independently, even in unpredicted communication situations in the future.
- Benesch (1996) criticizes the conventional needs analysis as being biased and designed for in – group wishes.
- Benesch (1996), Pennycook (1997), Benesch (2001), Hyland & Hamp-Lyons (2002) challenge the role of ESP as a medium that helps students develop skills and knowledge indispensable for functioning in their target environment. They argue that the learners accept the communicative norms existing in the target

environment uncritically, which may result in affecting students' needs to suit established norms in the particular professional environment and consequently maintaining practices and norms, not all of which may be enviable. Fostering critical awareness may better suit their needs and eventually facilitate access to their selected target environment.

2.2 The ESP practitioner

2.2.1 The roles of the ESP teacher

Being an ESP teacher is not an easy task. Many researchers such as Hutchinson & Waters 1987), Robinson (1991) and Jackson (1998) claim that to achieve success in ESP teaching a teacher must be creative, resourceful, and flexible. S/he should have good cross-communication, interpersonal and decision – making skills. Moreover, s/he should be a good time manager and leader. All of these can, however, be attributed to any good English teacher, not exclusively to ESP teachers.

It might be reasonable to claim that the borderline between the roles of ESP teacher and General English teacher are starting to dissipate. For example, Celani (2008) advocates a new approach in General English teaching which refers to Canagarajah's (2005) concept of *glocal knowledge* of the teacher (defined as global knowledge within a local context). Teachers (not only ESP teachers) are required to be:

> … researchers of their own practice, materials producers, evaluators, experimenters of new approaches, explorers of reality, syllabus builders, teachers of not only language but also of strategies, builders of social contexts inside and outside the classroom, open to change, adaptable, ready to continuously review their own practice."
>
> Celani (2008:419)

The above definition of the General English teacher does not appear to be very distant from the term **"ESP practitioner"** provided by Dudley-Evans & St. John much earlier. Dudley-Evans & St. John (1998:13-14) employ the term "ESP practitioner" instead of "ESP teacher" as they argue that the ESP teacher's work involves much more than teaching. The following key roles of the ESP practitioner are enumerated:

- teacher,
- course designer and materials provider,
- researcher,

- evaluator,
- collaborator.

The ESP practitioner as teacher

The methodology changes as the teaching becomes more specific. In the case of ESP classes, the teacher is no longer a "primary knower". In the case of very specific courses, the students themselves are frequently the primary knowers of the carrier content of the material. The teacher's main role is to generate real, authentic communication in the classroom on the basis of the students' knowledge.

The ESP practitioner as course designer and materials provider

Due to the lack of materials for ESP courses – the more specialized the course, the greater the rarity of teaching materials – one of the ESP teacher's roles is planning the course and providing materials for it. Provision does not only mean choosing materials and making a suitable number of copies for the class. The teacher's task also includes adapting material when published materials are unsuitable, or writing his/her own materials.

The ESP practitioner as researcher

An ESP teacher should also be a researcher to fulfill the students' needs. First of all, s/he should research the aims which they want to achieve. Then research is necessary to design a course, to prepare the teaching materials, and to determine the ESP students' particular interests.

The ESP practitioner as collaborator

By this term Dudley-Evans & St. John mean cooperating with subject specialists. From their perspective, this might be a simple form of cooperation in which the ESP teacher gains information about the subject syllabus, or tasks the students are required to carry out in their professional environment, or a stronger form of collaboration in which there is an integration between specialist studies or activities and the language.

The ESP practitioner as evaluator

Evaluation is not a new function and it is performed in General English classes too. Nevertheless, in the case of ESP, its role appears to be quite crucial. Apart from testing students, which is the most common type of evaluation, evaluation of the course and teaching materials is indispensable. General English courses have been well-studied and improved by a group of methodology specialists, whereas ESP courses are often tailor-made and unique, so that it is not feasible to prepare and design the course in order to satisfy all the ESP students' needs, as they are likely to change with each ESP course.

2.2.2 Subject knowledge dilemma

One of the most discussed issues related to ESP teacher's roles is the question of ESP teachers' subject knowledge (Sifakis 2003, Belcher 2006, Wu & Badger 2009) - how to deal with content with which ESP teachers are not completely familiar. In the earlier literature (McDonough 1984, Hutchinson & Waters 1987) there was a belief that ESP teachers do not have to acquire specialist subject knowledge - a knowledge of the fundamental principles of the subject area was considered sufficient. Nevertheless, it was considered advisable to take advantage of the learners' specialist knowledge and to ask for clarification of terminology and key concepts that the teacher did not know or /and understand.

There is still little research exploring how far ESP teachers' subject knowledge should extend. Wu & Badger (2009) cite Grossman (1990) and Ferguson (1997: 85) while describing the framework of ESP teachers' subject knowledge. Grossman (1990) defines it as contextual knowledge by which s/he means, what teachers know about their own role in the classroom and about their learners. Ferguson (1997:85), on the other hand, identifies three areas of such knowledge. These are:

- knowledge of the discipline's culture and values (excluding the actual content of the subject),
- knowledge of the epistemological basis of different disciplines (a type of knowledge which is philosophical in character),
- knowledge of genre and discourse, which is mainly linguistic in nature.

Others scholars like Kim (2006), Harding (2007), and Sesˇek (2007) are rather more vague and note that the ESP teachers' role is "understanding the nature of the material of the ESP specialism", being able to function in a variety of teaching contexts, to change university classroom formats and teaching methods. Concurrently, they advocate that teacher training programmes should be available enabling candidates to specialise in teaching ESP and for appropriate institutional support to be available.

Another disputed issue is the distinction between ESP teachers' knowledge of the subject and that of the subject specialist. Some researchers such as Jordan (1997:251) and Wu & Badger (2009) remark that it is a convoluted task to attempt to make a distinction between pedagogic content and subject matter knowledge. This view is confirmed by Howe (1993:148) who reports a conflict between herself as a teacher of English for academic legal purposes and a law teacher, over who should explain the phrase "time immemorial" to students, with the law teacher's famous comment: "You teach them the English, Mrs Howe, and we'll teach them the law". This depicts the common attitude of subject specialists towards ESP teaching, who believe that learners should be taught the skills of English for General Academic Purposes (EGAP) and not the content of English for Specific Academic Purposes (ESAP).

Barron (2002:298) completes the picture of unsuccessful (as he calls it) collaborative ventures between language and subject specialists, by presenting the three areas where failures may appear:

- the issues of different teaching methods and managing the process of collaboration,
- the issues of ''carrier content''(the subject matter of an exercise) and ''real content'' (the language or skill content of an exercise) - defined by Dudley-Evans & St. John 1998:11 and subordination of EAP teachers to subject content,
- the issues of the status of disciplinary entities and boundaries.

2.2.3 Co-operative teaching

Many researchers such as Barron (1992), Jordan (1997), Dudley-Evans (2001), Barron (2002), Kim (2006), Northcott & Brown (2006) and Bacha & Bahous (2008) share the concern about the distorted co-operation, which often puts language specialists in a subordinate position, and advocate for establishing a framework of co-operation between language and subject specialists, which would enhance their relationships and contribute to better language acquisition and raising literacy for a purpose on the part of the students.

A detailed overview of such co-operative teaching is provided by Barron (1992) who distinguishes four methods of working with colleagues in other departments:

- the subject – specialist informant (SSI) method,
- the consultative method,

- collaborative teaching,
- team – teaching.

As Barron (1992) notes the **SSI method** may be employed at all stages in ESP. It is used to determine the use of specific language points in one genre of a particular subject. The role of subject-specialists informants is to

> "provide the naïve ESP teacher with insights on the content and organization of texts and processes of their subjects (…) like unfamiliar artefacts in a subject that is completely alien to them."
>
> Barron (1992:2-3).

The consultative method is used when the content of the subject is determined by the ESP course designers and the subject specialist serves as a consultant at specific stages in a project to maintain content correctness.

In **collaborative teaching** the ESP teacher and the subject specialist cooperate on all aspects of the course such as course planning, teaching and assessment but do not share the classroom. The ESP teacher teaches the language and communication skills and the subject teacher teaches the concepts and other skills needed. The method aims at integrating content (determined by the subject department, not a foreign or ESP unit) and providing regular supervision of the situation at all stages by both language and subject specialists.

The true **team teaching** (as Barron calls it – intervention) occurs when the two teachers (language and subject specialists) are not only present in the classroom at all or most times but the whole course including syllabus design, materials, methodology and assessment is determined by both of them. The method is implemented where the mixture of skills and content would be too complicated and specialized for one person alone.

Barron (1992: 8-9) and Buckley (1998) present a discussion over the benefits and shortcomings of various co-operative teaching methods. As far as the benefits are concerned they stress that:

- the teachers can find out what they do not know from the experts,
- interdisciplinary relations between ESP or any foreign language departments and subject units may be promoted

which again may have tangible results such as joint projects and publications,
- subject teacher's language or even content subject syllabus may be modified to make it more understandable to students during lectures and seminars,
- students' awareness that there is a direct relationship between their subject, course, specialization and English may be fostered which again leads to more elaborate language skills and achieving more advanced levels of proficiency in language.

Some threats associated with team teaching are also mentioned. These are:
- the danger that ESP teachers may believe in all they hear from the subject specialists, who may also be wrong,
- timetabling problems may occur when two or more staff members need to be in the same classroom,
- subject specialists and ESP teachers may represent two very different pedagogic methods which may result in conflicts and misunderstanding,
- it is often difficult to persuade the authorities to introduce team teaching due to extensive costs.

Despite the fact that co-operative teaching methods are flexible and can be used with ESP students of different levels, countries, interests and subjects, such teaching is not prominent in ESP. This is due to the lack of tradition and guidelines, along with the reluctance of not only language teachers and subject specialists, but also user-institutions that find them too expensive and not cost-effective.

3. Language issues in ESP

3.1 The role of grammar and vocabulary in ESP

The issue of grammar in ESP is quite neglected in the literature as it is frequently believed that teaching ESP is not concerned with grammar.

Dudley-Evans & St. John (1998:74-80) have provoked a discussion over the importance of grammar in ESP teaching stating that grammatical difficulties and deficiencies may hinder the acquisition of productive and receptive skills in ESP. They enumerate five key grammatical forms that may pose impediments. These are:

- verbs and tense,
- voice,
- articles,
- nominalisation,
- logical connectors.

As far as **verbs and tenses** are concerned, Dudley-Evans & St. John (1998) emphasize that the use of tenses in ESP texts to a large extent relates to the text types and their sections. *Simple present, present perfect, simple past*, active and passive voice and the modal verbs generally dominate.

Another misconception in ESP teaching, as they comment, is the preponderance of the **passive voice** over the **active voice**. They cite Wingard (1981) who found that in the corpus of medical writing that he examined, 60% of the verbs were in the active voice whereas 40% in the passive. As Dudley-Evans & St. John (1998) remark, the usage of the passive or active voice does not depend on the type of writing, but is constrained by functional considerations i.e. the passive voice is widely used by writers to refer to previous research in their field, whereas the active voice is exploited for the writers' own research.

Modals such as *may, might, could* or *would* serve to express "the degree of certainty of a writer's commitment to a statement or claim" (Dudley-Evans & St. John, 1998:76). This concept of cautious language is called *hedging* and as Skelton (1988 quoted in Jordan, 1997:241) stresses, helps students "to achieve greater delicacy of meaning".

Dudley-Evans & St. John (1998) find two uses of **articles** particularly significant in ESP i.e. the absence of an article (0 article) and the use of '*the*' with named methods, procedures or cycles etc.. They underline that focusing on a limited number of uses is much more effective than the analysis of all uses.

Nominalisation i.e. the exploitation of verbal nouns usually ending in suffixes such as *- ment, -ness, -ation, -ition* is used to load a phrase which is simple from a grammatical point of view with complex information so that it can be picked up in the subject of the subsequent sentence.

Although as Dudley-Evans & St. John (1998) remark, **logical connectors**, such as *moreover, however, therefore* are slightly over-emphasized in ESP teaching materials, their importance should not be questioned as they enhance understanding of logical relationships and improve the acquisition of the four skills in ESP. Dudley-Evans & St. John (1998:80) also comment that different ESP contexts require diverse uses of grammar and the role of the ESP teacher is “to be sensitive to these contexts”.

The significance of vocabulary in ESP teaching is not in doubt. It may refer to understanding, learning and expanding specialised vocabulary, appropriate use of words and expressions in context, or revising and preparing to solve examination tasks.

Within this perspective two questions need to be posed:

- *Which vocabulary should be taught/learnt?*
- *How should it be taught/learnt?*

Which vocabulary should be taught/learnt?

Nation (2003) distinguishes four types of vocabulary: high frequency words, academic vocabulary, low frequency words and proper nouns.

High frequency words (also called the core vocabulary) constitute a comparatively limited number of words that are more frequent and useful in a wide range of language uses than other words in the language. The core 2,000–3,000 words are considered the basis of about 80% of all words used (Carter 1987). The words are usually selected on their familiarity and usefulness. Four criteria suggested by Sinclair and Renouf (1988) may be employed to select the core vocabulary. These are:

- the commonest word forms in the language,
- their central pattern of usage,
- the combinations which they typically form.

Academic vocabulary (also called technical vocabulary) constitutes 8.5%-10% coverage of the text and consists of words which occur across a number of disciplines i.e. about 570 word families. This vocabulary is quite central to learn the words from the specialised field of study.

Low frequency words (also called subject-core vocabulary) express the words of a particular discipline and although they cover only 5% of the text they encapsulate about 11,000 word families. Considering these large numbers, it is the responsibility of language teachers, as Nation (1990) emphasizes, to prepare learners to deal with them.

How should vocabulary be taught/learnt?

According to Nation (2001), the way vocabulary is taught/learnt in any form of language teaching should follow a set of principles. These principles should affect three major issues:

- content and sequencing,
- format and presentation,
- monitoring and assessment.

As far as the principles of **content choice and sequencing** are concerned, Nation (2001:385) advocates the use of available word lists (e.g. Coxhead, 1998, *Academic Word List*) to select the high-frequency and academic words to focus on. He points out, however, following the earlier remarks by Sinclair and Renouf's (1988) that:

- although the frequency of words is the most important criterion for the selection of words to be taught, the teacher should not only relate to frequency of word forms but also to the frequency of the various meanings,
- the introduction of lexical sets is against the criterion of frequent use,
- high frequency words have many diverse meanings thus the teacher should also have information about the frequency of their meanings.

Considering **format and presentation** a teacher should promote direct and indirect vocabulary learning (with the emphasis on the latter, as "contact with language in use should be given more time than decontextualised activities" Nation, 2001:388) and evaluate the quality of the teaching and learning techniques which facilitate repetition, retrieval or thoughtful processing. Bearing this in mind, a variety of techniques is indispensable to motivate and stimulate students. While selecting techniques, Nation (2001) refers to concepts such as **form** (e.g. reading aloud or peer teaching), **meaning** (e.g. answering questions or making word maps) and **use** (e.g. matching or finding collocates).

Monitoring and assessment in the form of teacher's observations, short-term and long-term achievement tests help to monitor learners' progress, identify the areas in the course content which require modification, determine vocabulary size and later assess how well and how much vocabulary has been learnt, and finally help to plan the next course.

The teaching of vocabulary in ESP follows similar principles to those which are employed in General English classes as the processes of deducting the meaning of vocabulary from the context or storing and retrieving new words in these two strands do not differ. What an ESP teacher should bear in mind, however, is that in some situations, learners starting an ESP course are often unfamiliar with academic vocabulary and need the teacher's assistance.

Register, Discourse and Genre Analysis

Research on the language which is subject-specific has been conducted since the 1960s commencing with analyzing register, then discourse and more recently genre. The term **register analysis** derived from the assumption that even though the grammar of particular specialisms does not differ, certain grammatical and lexical forms are exploited much more frequently than in General English. Register analysis operated almost exclusively at word and sentence level and took the form of statistical analyses into the frequencies of verbs, tenses and vocabulary for different ESP subjects to provide grammar registers and lexicons of those subjects. However, as Songhori (2008) points out, the concept was not free from shortcomings. Firstly, it was limited to the analysis of the text at the word and sentence level. Moreover, it was descriptive in character and did not explain anything. Finally, it lacked authenticity of text as materials produced in compliance with register analysis followed a similar pattern. Those deficiencies brought about the development of discourse analysis.

Discourse analysis related to describing the language and its organisation that is longer than a sentence e.g. paragraphs or complete texts and contrary to register analysis which examined the lexical and grammatical properties of register, it concentrated on the communicative values of discourse. However, as some researchers (West, 1998; Songhori, 2008:18) comment, the analysis was incomplete and limited to identification of the functional components of discourse at sentence level, yet did not provide any precise guidance on "how functions and sentences/utterances fit together to form text".

The research on language description and organisation led to a new concept i.e. **genre analysis**, which in a nutshell can be described as "the study of how language is used within a particular setting." (Jordan, 1997:231). The term "genre" was first used by Swales (1981) who expanded it to the following definition:

> "a genre comprises a class of communicative events, the members of which share some set of communicative purposes. These purposes are recognised be the expert members of the parent discourse community, and thereby constitute the rationale for the genre. This rationale shapes the schematic structure of the discourse and influences and constrains choice of content and styles (...) exemplars of a genre exhibit various patterns of similarity in terms of structure, style, content and intended audience."
> Swales (1990:58)

Swales (1990) proposes three key concepts in genre analysis: discourse community, genre, language learning, of which **discourse community** seems to be the critical element in the explanation of "genre". Paltridge (2006:24) defines discourse community as

> "a group of people who share some kind of activity (...) and have particular ways of communicating with each other. They generally have shared goals and may have shared values and beliefs".

As Johns (2004) and Hamps-Lyons (2011) remark, discourse communities are crucial to explaining the differences and patterns between disciplines and within disciplines. Discourse communities are built by their members and "membership is always in influx" (Hamps-Lyons 2011:95). They are not static and transform as the world changes to produce utterances appropriate to specific situations. This way, as Hamps-Lyons (2011:95) remarks, "we are much better able to understand how academic language and interaction work **within** disciplines, and to begin to understand which differences are significant and why".

The issue of genre analysis is also extensively exploited by Bhatia (1993, 2002, 2004) and Bhatia & Gotti (2006). Bhatia remarks that genre analysis may also serve as a

> " pedagogically effective and convenient tool for the design of language teaching programmes, often situated within simulated contexts of classroom activities" Bhatia (2002:3).

The specificity of Legal English

Most researchers (Bloor & Bloor, 1986; Corder, 1993; Basturkmen, 2006) perceive **language for specific purposes** from two perspectives. One perspective presents all language as one variety or another i.e. all languages are learned in some context or another. A different perspective refers to the basic core of general language perceived as the common core plus a common set of grammatical and other characteristics that learners need to acquire before they study ESP (Bloor & Bloor, 1986; Corder, 1993; Pieńkos, 1999; Coxhead & Nation, 2001; Basturkmen, 2006). Registers of language use such as Legal, Business or Technical English can be termed "**variety**". As Davies (2001) comments:

> "varieties exhibit a lack both of discreteness and of coherence. 'Medical English', for example, overlaps with 'chemical English', on the one hand, and, on the other, 'medical English' is itself made up of the English of surgery, the English of general medicine, the English of paediatrics and so on." Davies (2001:137)

As far as Legal discourse is concerned Jopek-Bosiacka (2008:44-86) acknowledges its five characteristic features. They are:

- **accuracy/precision–**many legal texts such as contracts or regulations contain a special section where particular terms and expressions are explained to avoid ambiguity:

  For the purposes of this Directive:
  (...) 2) "Family member" means:
  (a) the spouse;
  (b) the partner with whom the Union citizen has contracted a registered partnership, on the basis of the legislation of a Member State, if the legislation of the host Member State treats registered partnerships as equivalent to marriage and in accordance with the conditions laid down in the relevant legislation of the host Member State;
  (c) the direct descendants who are under the age of 21 or are dependants and those of the spouse or partner as defined in point (b);
  (d) the dependent direct relatives in the ascending line and those of the spouse or partner as defined in point (b);

  Extract from Article 2 of the Directive on the Right of Citizens of the Union and their Family Members to Move and Reside Freely within the Territory of the Member States (Directive 2004/38/EC)

- **ambiguity** i.e. lack of clarity in language; as in the example provided by Schane (2006:12-53); The sentence: *The chicken is too hot to eat.* may have at least four different meanings:

  The live chicken is feeling excessively warm and doesn't want to eat.
  The live chicken is highly aroused sexually and not in the mood to eat.
  The chicken as food is just off the grill, is sizzling, and is unable to be eaten now.
  The chicken as food is excessively spicy and therefore unable to be eaten.

Schane (2006:12-53), in his book, provides a thorough overview of ambiguity in language and misunderstanding in law.

- **specialisation (special terminology)** i.e. common words with uncommon meanings e.g. *instrument = legal document; party = person contracting or litigating*,
- **conservatism** i.e. the usage of archaic structures and expressions which derive from Latin (e.g. *versus, quorum, inter alia*), French (e.g. *force majeure, lien, verdict*) or Anglo-Saxon English (e.g. *hereby, thereof, herein*),
- **complexity** – at the level of words (e.g. *null and void*), sentences (passive vs. active voice, nominalisation) or at the sentence level (lack of punctuation marks).

Even though in some cases, specificity and complexity of language variety can be valued (as in the study of poetry) with reference to Legal English, this complexity and uncertainty poses obstacles in teaching and learning:

- legal discourse has its own specificity which is profoundly affected by ethics, philosophy, history, religions and even the culture of a particular nation (Northcott & Brown, 2006),
- legal discourse is hardly ever identical from one country to another; some discrepancies result from differences in institutions and lack of equivalents between common law jurisdictions and civil law jurisdictions or political systems e.g. *solicitor* lacks the equivalent in Polish, *zachowek* or *spółdzielnia mieszkaniowa* lacks the equivalent in English (Badger, 2003; Wagner, 2003),
- legal discourse seems to be isolated from the rest of common language,
- legal English constitutes a problematic field due to "the close interplay and content" (Northcott & Brown, 2006:360),
- lack of teaching materials or resources for Legal English teachers; on the basis of Candlin *et al.*'s research (2002) it can be stated that most materials in Legal English are aimed at native speakers of English and are written with the assumption that the learner (the reader) is at least familiar with the socio-cultural context, such as the country's system of government, historical and cultural values,
- the prepared materials are frequently developed for a particular audience in a particular country and often irrelevant for audiences from a different country (Candlin *et al.* 2002)

- lack of guidelines for Legal English teachers who frequently do not possess a legal background and legal terminology, which makes the process of teaching Legal English extremely stressful and challenging,
- specificity of legal discourse (mentioned above) such as: Latinisms, long and complex sentences, double negations, common terms with uncommon legal meanings, extensive use of the passive voice or a high degree of formality (Gibbons, 2004; Haigh, 2004; Ingels, 2006),
- teaching Legal English often requires very close co-operation with the subject – specialists (Barron, 1992; Northcott & Brown, 2006) who are frequently reluctant to help.

For the reasons presented above teachers of English both in Poland and abroad, although they recognise the importance of Legal English in the contemporary world and a significant number of its discourse community i.e. legal professionals, often treat teaching English for Legal Purposes as "hot potato" game –would resign or give it up if they could or did not have to do it.

***

ESP appears to be gaining in popularity and acquiring a new dimension in many countries. An increasing number of people find their General English satisfactory and desire to learn the language of their professional domain as they believe it will bring them improved job prospects in the future. There are some aspects of ESP teaching that can be both a hindrance and a challenge for ESP teachers. These include the lack of an ESP tradition and guidelines and lack of specialist knowledge. Hutchinson & Waters (1987) describe the first problem as the lack of orthodoxy – by which they mean the lack of a long tradition that might have given some stability and guidelines for the practice. They state that this problem has its origin in the relatively brief existence of ESP. The discussions over the term "special" in the phrase "ESP" or the debates over the relevance of ESP methodology show this lack of orthodoxy. Another aspect that requires thorough consideration is the change in the role of a language teacher in ESP classes. S/he ceases being the "primary knower" and is equipped with more functions and responsibilities and is frequently expected (by ESP learners) to possess specialist knowledge. The learners, or more precisely, their needs affect the course (and syllabus) design, the way ESP materials are selected or developed and the way in which progress is assessed or tested.

CHAPTER TWO

SYLLABUS DESIGN FOR ESP

1. Key issues in syllabus design

1.1 The definition and the roles of a syllabus

In the earlier literature researchers could not reach agreement on what a "syllabus" is. Some scholars (Allen, 1984:61; Stern, 1984:10-11; Widdowson, 1984:26; Nunan, 1988:6) drew a clear distinction between syllabus design and methodology. In this sense "syllabus" was seen as the selection and grading content, "methodology", on the other hand, was concerned with the selection of learning tasks and activities. In a broader context the definition was criticized by other researchers [Breen (1984:49), Yalden (1984:14), Candlin (1984:32)] who argued that in the case of communicative language teaching, the distinction between content and tasks is not so evident.

Hutchinson & Waters (1987:80-84), on the other hand, claim that when defining "a syllabus" it is crucial to be explicit as to what kind of syllabus we have in mind. They refer to their concept of various syllabus types, remarking that there are several different ways in which a syllabus can be defined and there is no necessary relationship between any of the different kinds of syllabus.

They provide the following types of syllabuses:

- **the evaluation syllabus** – reflects an official assumption as to the nature of language and linguistic performance,
- **the organizational syllabus** – as in the case of the evaluation syllabus, this reflects suppositions as to the nature of language and linguistic performance but additionally takes into consideration the nature of learning,
- **the materials syllabus** – the materials writer as the first interpreter adjoins some assumptions to the previous models –s/he decides, for example, about the context, the number

and type of exercises to be devoted to a particular aspect of language etc.,

- **the teacher syllabus** – similar to the materials syllabus, here the teacher is the second interpreter after the materials writer, affecting the image that the learners receive,
- **the classroom syllabus –** understood as a dynamic and interactive environment with its own particular factors e.g. a visitor or tired students generate their own syllabus,
- **the learner syllabus** – perceived as an internal syllabus and a kind of filter through which learners see other syllabuses.

McDonough & Shaw (1993), Jordan (1997) in defining the concept of "syllabus" follow the approach which makes a distinction between content and methodology. A syllabus may be described as:

> "the overall organizing principle for what is to be taught and learnt, (…) general statement as to the pedagogical arrangement of learning content"
>
> McDonough & Shaw (1993:10)

> "a specification of what is to be included in a language course (…) and entails the selection, grading and sequencing of the language and other content, and the division of content into units of manageable material; the methodology employed in implementing the syllabus will include materials selection and development (…) and will involve a selection of the learning tasks, activities and exercise types, and how they are to be presented, in a particular environment, for teaching and learning; it will conclude with assessment and evaluation"
>
> Jordan (1997:56)

Rabbani's (2006) definition of "a syllabus" is comparatively elaborate and encapsulates both the content and the methodology. "A syllabus" is defined as:

> "an overall plan of the learning process; it must specify what components, or learning items, must be available, or learned by a certain time; what is the most efficient sequence in which they are learned; what items can be learned simultaneously; what items are available from the stock, and the whole process is determined by consideration of how long it takes to produce or learn a component or item".
>
> Rabbani (2006:3)

Syllabus vs. curriculum

The terms "syllabus" and "curriculum" often cause confusion as they are used in a different way on either side of the Atlantic. In Great Britain "syllabus'' is described as the content or subject matter of particular subjects while "curriculum" stands for the totality of content to be taught and aims to be fulfilled within one school or educational system. In the USA "curriculum" seems to be close to the British meaning of "syllabus".

Following Graves' (1996) and Rabbani's (2006) definitions we can say that "curriculum' is a very general concept, which involves consideration of the whole complex of philosophical, social and administrative factors, which contribute to the planning of an educational programme. "Syllabus", on the other hand, refers to the subpart of a curriculum, which is concerned with a specification of content to be taught.

The role of syllabus

The role of syllabus can be seen from a multidimensional perspective. The most elaborate description of its functions is provided by Grunert (1997). She stresses that a syllabus:

- establishes a point of contact and connection between students and the teacher by providing basic information such as the name, address, telephone numbers etc.,
- expresses the teacher's attitudes toward students, learning and teaching process,
- presents the teacher's beliefs about educational purposes (whether the course is product or process oriented, expectations towards students, goals and objectives, learning strategies and techniques used),
- outlines the agenda of the course,
- collects required handouts to be used during the course by students,
- defines students' responsibilities so they can manage their time effectively and gain control over their learning process,
- describes active learning which is perceived as taking an active role in acquiring correct information,
- aids students to evaluate their readiness for the language course (like what they should already know or what skills they should have before the course),
- sets the course in a wider perspective, presenting teachers as researchers engaged in their professional activity i.e. this way students could be encouraged to participate in a

community of scholars and also be shown how the course "fits within the discipline or profession, the general program of study, and their own educational plans",

- provides a conceptual framework, understood as major issues, topics, key questions, which may facilitate students in organizing their learning process,
- describes available learning aids,
- expresses the role of technology in the course, as an indispensable tool to access information and enhance communication with each other or monitoring and reflection on their progress in learning,
- can expand to provide supplementary reading materials, which are not included in course texts, or not obtainable with ease,
- can advance the effectiveness of student note taking but outlining the topics for lectures and presentations, the things the teacher wants students to remember; this way providing an opportunity for students' own interpretation and elaboration of the material,
- can include material which supports learning outside the classroom, by students with strategies which facilitate their work with supplementary materials,
- can serve as a learning contract which defines mutual obligations between the teacher and students, and also may express the viewpoint of user-institution.

However, in a different approach, Parkes & Harris (2002) regard the role of a syllabus in a more concise way. A syllabus is: **a contract**, **a permanent record** and **a learning tool**. A syllabus as **a contract** refers to the overall framework and requirements of the course which constitute an agreement between students and their instructor. The framework and requirements denote various responsibilities such as attendance, assignments, examinations etc. A syllabus as **a permanent record** provides documentary evidence of the course: with reference to the material covered, the level and the scope of the course and the kinds of credit. A syllabus as **a learning tool** is understood as an aid whose aim is to support student learning, which is comprised of traditional syllabus components, study tips, learning resources or tests.

Their notion is not new, however. It is based on Matejka & Kurke's concept of syllabus functions. Matejka & Kurke (1994:115-117) identified four distinct purposes of a syllabus. They perceive it as a **contract** (agreement between the teacher and students), a **communicative device** (effective presentation of the teacher's thoughts and answers to students' anticipated questions), a **plan** (the arrangement of actions for the course) and a **cognitive map** ("the teacher is the guide and the only one with the cognitive map of the destination").

However, these multifunctional aspects of a syllabus, as Hutchinson & Waters (1987) point out, are not free of dangers. It is crucial to note that a syllabus is a model understood as a teaching ideal - a syllabus is an approximate statement of what will be *taught* not what will be *learnt,* as it does not comprise unsubstantial factors such as personalities, motivation, emotions and individual differences.

1.2 Types of syllabuses

There are diverse types of syllabuses that may be implemented in a language course. The discussion on syllabus types started with Wilkins' (1976) binary distinction between synthetic and analytic syllabuses. According to Wilkins' (1976) definition:

> "in **synthetic syllabuses**, the content of instruction is organized in terms of the target language's grammar, pronunciation, vocabulary, etc. This content is pre-selected and taught incrementally until the whole language is covered. The learner's task is to re-synthesize the language that has been broken down into a large number of small pieces with the aim of making this learning task easier. (…) in contrast **analytic syllabuses** are organized in terms of the purposes for which people are learning language and the kinds of language performance that are necessary to meet those purposes"
>
> Wilkins (1976:2, 13)

R.V. White (1988) provides another classification of syllabus which relies on the distinction of two syllabus types: Type A and Type B. This division partially covers the synthetic and analytic distinction presented by Wilkins (1976). The main assumptions are presented in the form of a table given below.

Type A: What is to be learnt?	Type B: How is it to be learnt?
Interventionist	Non-interventionist
External to the learner	Internal to the learner
Other directed	Inner directed or self fulfilling
Determined by authority	Negotiated between learners and teachers
Teacher as decision-maker	Learner and teacher as joint decision makers
Content = what the subject is to the expert	Content = what the subject is to the learner
Content = a gift to the learner from the teacher or knower	Content = what the learner brings and wants
Objectives defined in advance	Objectives described afterwards
Assessment by achievement or by mastery	Assessment in relationship to learners' criteria of success
Doing things to the learner	Doing things for or with the learner.

Table 2-1. Language Syllabus Design: Two Types (White 1988:44-45)

E. Spector-Cohen *et al.* (2001:373-374) provide a comprehensive overview of advantages and disadvantages of both types.

	Advantages	Disadvantages
Type A	• improves vocabulary acquisition • improves the rate of learning • provides explicit knowledge for gradual mastery of language "a rationale for sequencing thus learning and teaching appears to be systematic" • some focus on discrete language elements also exists in L1	• learning may seem inauthentic as the mode of learning is far from how L1 spoken language is acquired • may not take into account the learner's specific needs sufficiently • aims for idealized native language model • students may not always be able to "ultimately re-synthesize the language into an integrated whole system"

Type B	• learners are exposed to authentic target language situations • there is a focus on communicative tasks not on grammatical forms of the language • equips learners with skills more efficiently • could facilitate "a bridge from *declarative knowledge* (knowledge about the facts and things we know) to *procedural knowledge"* (knowledge that consists of the things we know how to do)	• may require a certain level of linguistic proficiency, therefore, may not be appropriate for students at low L2 proficiency level • no clear rationale for sequencing nature and number of the various tasks in the course • as it is based on learners' needs analysis a teacher may find it difficult to provide ready-made suitable materials thus s/he is required to prepare more and also design course materials

Table 2-2. Advantages and disadvantages of Type A and Type B syllabuses

Nunan's taxonomy (1988) takes an important stand in the discussion on syllabus types. It is based on the distinction between **product** and **process syllabuses**. The former focus on the knowledge and skills which learners should gain in the learning process, the latter concentrate on the learning experiences themselves. Within the product-oriented syllabuses he follows Wilkins'(1976) syllabus division into synthetic and analytic ones. Nunan discusses two syllabus types within synthetic syllabuses: **grammatical** and **functional–notional** ones. The former type is considered to be the most common syllabus type. It consists of items selected and graded according to grammatical simplicity and complexity. It derives from the assumption that language comprises a finite set of rules which can be learned one by one. The latter one (the functional–notional syllabus) consists of functions that are performed when language is used (e.g. requesting) or of the notions that language is used to express e.g. time. Within process –oriented syllabuses both **procedural** and **task based syllabuses** consist of the specification of the tasks and activities that learners will do in class and focus on the classroom process which stimulates learning. **A content syllabus**, on the other hand derives from some well–defined subject area.

These considerations over the different syllabus types were taken up again by Long & Crookes (1992:1) who expanded Wilkins' (1976) classification which divides syllabuses into synthetic and analytic ones. They remark that synthetic syllabuses

> "rely on learner's assumed ability to learn language in parts independently of one another, and also integrate or synthesize the pieces when the time comes to use them for communicative purposes".

Structural, lexical, notional functional and most situational and topical syllabuses are synthetic syllabuses as acquisition of knowledge takes the form of gradual accumulation of separately taught parts, building up to the whole structure of the language.

As for analytic syllabuses, Long & Crookes (1992) update Wilkins's definition claiming that analytical syllabuses are those which present the target language whole chunks at a time, without linguistic interference or control. In their opinion procedural, process and task syllabuses are examples of the analytic syllabus type.

Long & Crookes (1992) also provide a detailed study of the analytical syllabuses i.e. three types of task-based approaches to course design presenting the key issues for each approach and possible shortcomings.

Syllabus type	**Key issues**
PROCEDURAL SYLLABUS	• associated with the work in India from 1979-84 of Prabhu Ramani and others on the Bangalore /Madras Communicational Teaching Project • language is acquired subconsciously through "the operation of some internal system of abstract rules and principles"(Prabhu, 1987:70) when the learner's attention is focused on meaning not language • students need plenty of opportunity to develop their comprehension abilities before any production is demanded of them • the basis of each lesson is a problem or a task • teacher speech accompanying use of a procedural syllabus is not preselected or structurally graded, but roughly tuned as a natural by-product of the spontaneous adjustments made to communicate with less proficient speakers inside or outside classroom • error correction: ungrammatical learner utterances are accepted for their content, although they may be reformulated by the teacher

PROCESS SYLLABUS	• focus on learner and learning processes and preferences • syllabus as a subject for negotiation and reinterpretation by teachers and learners • traditional conception of the syllabus (as an itemized list creating a repertoire of communication) replaced by a syllabus which promotes a learner's capacity for communication (Breen, 1984) • course design consists of providing the resources and materials needed for making general decisions, alternative procedures for making those decisions, alternative activities and alternative tasks
TASK-BASED (TBLT) SYLLABUS	• a needs identification is required in terms of the real-world target tasks learners are preparing to undertake • first target tasks are identified via the needs analysis, then they are classified into (target) tasks types, after that pedagogic tasks are derived from the task types and sequenced to form the task-based syllabus; in the classroom teachers and students actually work on pedagogic tasks • assessment of student learning by way of task-based criterion-referenced tests, whose focus is whether or not students can perform some task to criterion • compatible with research findings on language learning • a principled approach to content selection • an attempt to incorporate findings from classroom-centered research when making decisions concerning the design of materials and methodology

Table 2-3. Key issues in procedural, process and task-based syllabuses by Long & Crookes (1992)

Syllabus type	
PROCEDURAL SYLLABUS.	• as there is no task-based needs identification there is no rationale for the content of such a syllabus (i.e. task selection); in consequence it is not possible to verify the appropriacy of particular pedagogic tasks for a given group of learners • grading task difficulty and sequencing tasks both appear to be arbitrary process left partly to real-time impressionistic judgments by the classroom teacher • the absence of overt feedback on error is criticized and collects negative evidence and empirical findings on instructed interlanguage development, which support the need for a focus on form in language teaching
PROCESS SYLLABUS	• is not based on any prior needs identification, which raises problems for selection • in the case of grading task difficulty and sequencing tasks a variety of possible criteria are put forward without any resolution • no explicit provision is made for a focus on language form • it is not clear to what (if any) theory or research in SLA the process syllabus is to be held accountable
TBLT SYLLABUS	• limited research base • as a consequence of little empirical support available for the numerous suggested parameters of task classification and difficulty assessing task difficulty and sequencing pedagogic tasks becomes more problematic • the problem of finiteness of tasks,

Table 2-4. Possible shortcomings of procedural, process and task-based syllabuses by Long & Crookes (1992)

A comprehensive division of syllabus types is proposed by Jordan (1997:60) which encompasses the above–mentioned approaches. Jordan (1997:60) distinguishes three types of syllabuses:

- **Type a** (Content or Product) which focuses on the end result,
- **Type b** (Skills) which focuses on skills practised,

- **Type c** (Methods or Process) which focuses on the means to an end.

Type a:

- grammatical, structural/language form
- notional-functional
- situational
- topic
- content-based

A **grammatical syllabus** concentrates on aspects of grammar like verb tenses, adjectives, nouns or prepositions etc. and grades them for teaching apparently from simple to more complex, but also taking into consideration their usefulness and frequency.

A **notional-functional syllabus** (often called "the communicative approach") stresses communication and focuses on *notions* (e.g. time, space, quantity) and *functions* (i.e. communicative purposes like greetings or apologies).

A **situational syllabus** enumerates the situations and contexts in which the language is used and analyses the language necessary for these situations and the contexts like checking into a hotel, visiting a doctor etc.

A **topic syllabus** focuses on the topics selected from the students' studies and appropriate grammar and vocabulary. For example, for law students such topics might include: human rights, system of courts, sources of law etc..

A **content-based syllabus** comprises teaching students the language, skills and academic conventions connected with their particular field of study and its content (subject-matter).

Type b: Skills

A **skill-based syllabus** concentrates on one or more of the four traditional language skills. It may also converge on other skills such as learning skills, cognitive skills or communication skills.

Type c:

- Process
- Procedural/ task-based
- Learning-centred / negotiated

A **process syllabus** focuses on the learner and learning processes and preferences thus the final selection of the syllabus components (subject-matter, resources or learning purposes etc.) is made by students themselves.

A **procedural/task based syllabus** is based on "a task" or "a problem" and it aims at completing the task and focusing on meaning.

A **learning-centred / negotiated syllabus** also focuses on the learner who is responsible for making a number of decisions. As Bloor & Bloor (1988) remark as cited in Jordan (1997) the areas that might be negotiated are: various aspects of language use, target levels of competence or preferred study modes.

1.3 Selecting and grading syllabus content

Selecting and grading syllabus content is a task which a syllabus designer needs to consider cautiously in order to present the principles of teaching and learning on which the syllabus is based.

Komorowska (2006:36-38) advocates considering four criteria for content selection. These are:

- the criterion connected with **the basic discipline**
- the criterion of **durability of knowledge**
- the criterion of **content usefulness**
- the criterion of **learners' needs**

Dudley-Evans & St. John (1998:163) note that there are a lot of constraints, factors and variables to keep in mind to make a satisfactory syllabus (course) version. The most recurrent are:

- tutors (e.g. their experience and capabilities),
- students (their number, nationalities and language level),
- time (the length of the course, its frequency),
- facilities and equipment,
- finance (budget size, methods of payment),
- space (room size, location, furniture),
- motivation of students: their attitudes and expectations,
- past experience.

Criterion	The main characteristics
the criterion connected with the basic discipline	• objective and non- controversial • the content selected is considered the most crucial to remember or the most basic • the selection of content often depends not on the author of the curriculum but the academic representatives of the disciplines • not always practical as it does not take the learners' needs into account • might be too difficult for lower-level learners
the criterion of durability of knowledge	• objective and non - controversial • the content selected is considered durable, permanent and changes infrequently during knowledge acquisition • the learners are accustomed to the basic canon of knowledge • the newest and the most interesting aspects of knowledge connected with technology development and progress are excluded from the content • not always practical as it does not take learners' needs into the account • less attractive for learners
the criterion of content usefulness	• subjective and controversial • practical and attractive as it takes into account learners' needs • real content • motivational value • changeable and unpredictable • might be used with lower level students and for vocational courses
the criterion of learners' needs	• connected with expectations, level, motivation and interests of learners • motivation is the basis of the learners' efforts • subjective and controversial • real content • motivational value • changeable and unpredictable • often used for ESP courses

Table 2-5. The criteria of content selection by Komorowska (2006)

As far as grading syllabus content is concerned, Komorowska (2006:38) discusses four criteria that may be employed in the process. These are:

- The criterion of **academic discipline structure** – gradation of syllabus content follows a subject-specific syllabus,
- The criterion of **usefulness** – syllabus content is graded in accordance with the principle of usefulness of materials i.e. the most useful materials are exploited at the commencement of the course even if they are complex and boring,
- The criterion of **motivation** – grades the content according to its attractiveness for students,
- The criterion of **language acquisition** – the gradation of content follows the principle: from simple components of syllabus to more complex ones.

Jordan (1997), Dudley-Evans & St. John (1998) and Komorowska (2006) emphasize that selecting and grading content depends on balancing between different criteria to suit a particular context and circumstances. Dudley-Evans & St. John (1998:162) compare this to "a dynamic mix of juggling and doing puzzles" as syllabus designers frequently have to change and shift different elements until they form a satisfactory picture.

1.4 Syllabus evaluation

Wholey *et al.* (2010) define syllabus evaluation (they employ the term "program evaluation") as "the application of systematic methods to address questions about program operations and results." The concept of evaluation is completed by the framework for syllabus evaluation provided by Rea-Dickins & Germaine (1992:74), which comprises the following questions:

- Who is the information for?
- Why are we carrying out the evaluation?
- What will be evaluated? What aspects of the teaching and learning curriculum will be evaluated?
- What are the criteria to be used in the evaluation? Who establishes these criteria?
- When will the evaluation take place? What are the time scales for the evaluation?
- What procedures will be used to obtain the data?
- Who/Where are we going to get information from?
- Who are we going to involve in the evaluation?

- How are we going to manage the evaluation?
- What are we going to do with the information we get?
- What are the constraints and problems that need to be taken into account when planning for and implementing the evaluations?
- Are the evaluations effective?

In theory, there are many models for syllabus evaluation. A selection of some is presented below:

The CIPP model

The CIPP-Stufflebeam's model for evaluation is a comprehensive framework for conducting evaluations of programs, projects, products or evaluation systems. Stufflebeam & Shinkfield define evaluation as:

> "the process of delineating, obtaining, reporting, and applying descriptive and judgmental information about some object's merit, worth, significance, and probity in order to guide decision making, support accountability, disseminate effective practices, and increase understanding of the involved phenomena."
>
> Stufflebeam & Shinkfield (2007:326)

The acronym CIPP denotes the model's core concepts which include: Context (C), Input (I), Process (P), Product (P). **Context** evaluations assess problems, needs, opportunities to facilitate a decision – making process in estimating and judging goals, priorities and results. **Input** evaluations judge alternative approaches, action and staff plans budgets and its cost-effectiveness along with feasibility to achieve assumed targets and goals. Implementation of the plans which help staff to perform activities and users judge program implementation and outcomes interpretations is assessed by **process** evaluation. **Product** evaluation estimates and assesses the outcomes of the program.

SWOT model

The strategic planning process in any company but also in a school or university means setting the objectives which an organization seeks to accomplished. To devise a strategy to meet these objectives, the organization's situation has to be analyzed. The SWOT analysis is a tool for accomplishing a situation analysis of this kind, as it allows the strengths (S) to be maximized, the weaknesses (W) to be minimized or eliminated, opportunities (O) to be taken advantage of (O) and threats (T) to be mitigated.

Pahl & Richter (2007:6) define the components of the analysis as follows:

- **Strengths** – capabilities that enable your company or unit to perform well,
- **Weaknesses** – characteristics that prohibit your company or unit from performing well and need to be addressed,
- **Opportunities** – trends, forces, events, and ideas that your company or unit can capitalize on,
- **Threats** – possible events or forces outside of your control that your company or unit needs to plan for or decide how to mitigate.

Classic evaluation model by R.W. Tyler

Evaluation in this approach assesses whether, and to what extent, the objectives set in the syllabus have been accomplished. Tyler *et al.* (1989) emphasize that Tyler's rationale is based on the belief that educators (teachers) must clarify and validate their objectives, develop learning experiences to help students to meet objectives and ultimately evaluate students' progress in attaining their objectives.

Tyler (1946:1) poses questions which he considers fundamental in developing any curriculum and plan of instruction. The questions are:

1. What educational purposes should the school seek to attain?
2. What educational experiences can be provided that are likely to attain these purposes?
3. How can these educational experiences be effectively organised?
4. How can we determine whether these purposes are being attained?

Evaluation is performed in the form of tests to check what students can or cannot do.

Action Research Model

Action research can be defined as any systematic inquiry conducted by teachers for collecting information on how they teach, and how their students learn. Mertel (2006:2) comments that it is done "*by* teachers *for* themselves" and "allows teachers to study their own classroom (...) to improve their quality and effectiveness." As Komorowska (2006:56), Mertel (2006:2) and Sagor (2007:4) highlight action research is a four - stage process, whose stages may differ to some extent:

Stage 1: The **Planning Stage** which typically encompasses the identification of a problem, collecting information, reviewing the associated literature and developing a research plan.
Stage 2: The **Acting Stage** which usually involves the implementation of the plan and collecting the data.
Stage 3: The **Developing Stage** during which the gathered data is analysed and an action plan is developed.
Stage 4: The **Reflecting Stage** where the results are disseminated, and finally, the research process is reflected upon.

2. Syllabus design for ESP

As mentioned above, ESP derives from the need to use language as a tool in facilitating success in professional life, and not as a hobby or an interest, therefore specifying the situations in which a learner will use the language is crucial. This objective is fulfilled by means of needs analysis which is, as Hutchinson & Waters (1987:54) claim,

> "the irreducible minimum of an ESP approach to course design …since it is the awareness of course design of a target situation that distinguishes the ESP learner from the learner of General English."

2.1 Needs Analysis

2.1.1 The definition and different approaches to Needs Analysis

Many scholars and authors (Munby, 1978; Hutchinson & Waters, 1987; Robinson, 1991; West, 1994; Jordan, 1997; Dudley – Evans & St. John, 1998; Deutch, 2003; Jeong 2005, Cowling 2007; Songhori, 2008; Akbari, 2011; Tsao, 2011; Lockwood, 2012) acknowledge that **needs analysis** (also known as needs assessment) plays a crucial role in designing and conducting any language course, not necessarily an ESP course. As Jeong (2005) remarks, the necessity for needs analysis arises from the assumption that "when language teaching is focused on what learners are interested in, language learning is most effective".

The Routledge Encyclopedia of Language Teaching and Learning (2004) defines the term "needs analysis" as:

> the process of gathering and interpreting information on the uses to which language learners will put the target language (TL) following instruction; and what the learners will need to do in the learning situation in order to

> learn the TL. The results of needs analyses are used in language programme planning to make decisions about appropriate learning objectives, syllabus content, teaching and assessment methods, learning materials and resources.

A similar definition is provided by Iwai *et al.* (1999) who regard a needs analysis as collecting information which helps to develop a syllabus which meets the needs of a particular group of students. Some scholars such as Brindley (1989), Berwick (1989), Spratt (1999), Deutch, 2003; Flowerdew (2005b), Jeong (2005), Taillefer (2007), Wozniak, 2010; Lockwood (2012) underline, however, that there are different types of needs and we should make a clear difference between needs identified by the teachers (course designers) and those expressed by learners.

This distinction raises the question how "**needs**" can be defined. The term is not uniform in the literature. Hutchinson & Waters (1987) make a distinction between **target needs** (what the learner needs to do in the target situation) and **learning needs** (what the learner needs to do in order to learn). Within target needs they distinguish necessities, lacks and wants. **Necessities** are understood as the needs that are determined by the demands of the target situation, **lacks** as the gap between the target proficiency and the existing proficiency of the learners, finally **wants** are described as the learners' views of their needs. Jordan (1997:22) additionally mentions "demands, likes, deficiencies, goals, aims, purposes and objectives".

A comprehensive overview of needs analysis in language teaching is provided by West (1994) who refers to its history, theoretical grounds and approaches to needs analysis. Songhori (2008) also presents an overview of the approaches to needs analysis, emphasizing that the concept of needs analysis should be treated as a jigsaw, where each approach is perceived as a piece which completes the picture.

Songhori (2008:3) lists the following terms with reference to needs analysis:

- Target Situation Analysis (TSA)
- Present Situation Analysis (PSA)
- Pedagogic Needs Analysis
    - Deficiency Analysis
    - Strategy Analysis or Learning Needs Analysis
    - Means Analysis
- Register Analysis

- Discourse Analysis
- Genre Analysis

Target Situation Analysis (TSA)

The scientific discussion over needs analysis started with the publication of Munby's Communicative Syllabus Design in 1978. Munby introduced the concept of a **"communicative needs processor"** which constitutes the basis of Munby's approach to needs analysis.

The term "Target Situation Analysis (TSA)" was introduced by Chambers (1980:29) based on Munby's work; he defined Target Situation Analysis (TSA) as "communication in the target situation". Investigation of the target situation helps to establish target needs and target level performance. Munby claimed that the following components are essential for the syllabus designer:

- *participant* - specified information relating to the learner's identity and language skills,
- *purposive domain* – the purposes for which the target language is needed,
- *setting* - the environment in which the target language will be used,
- *interaction* – the people with whom learner will be interacting,
- *instrumentality* – the medium, the mode and the channel,
- *dialect,*
- *target level,*
- *communicative event* – the productive and receptive skills the learner will need to master,
- *communicative key* – the interpersonal attitudes and tones the learner will be required to improve.
- to find "as thoroughly as possible the linguistic form a prospective ESP learner is likely to use in various situations in his target language"

Songhori (2008:4).

Researchers such as Hutchinson & Waters (1987), following Munby's model, provide a framework for TSA which comprises a list of questions the teacher should ask. They are the following:

- Why is the language needed?
- How will the language be used?
- What will the content areas be?

- Who will the learners use the language with?
- Where will the language be used?
- When will the language be used?

Some scholars (Hutchinson & Waters, 1987; West, 1994; Dudley – Evans & St. John, 1998) comment on the shortcomings of the TSA approach and Munby's model:

- it concentrates on the analysts' point of view, neglecting others (those of learners or user-institutions),
- it takes up a lot of time to conduct and enforce the model systematically and comprehensively,
- the factors in the analysis are not prioritised,
- no procedure is provided to convert the learner's profile into a language syllabus,
- the model collects data *about* the learner rather than *from* the learner,
- the model recommends considering some constraints after the needs analysis procedure whilst many researchers believe they should be thought over at the start of the needs analysis process.

Present Situation Analysis (PSA)

Robinson (1991), Jordan (1997) and Dudley – Evans & St. John (1998) perceive PSA as a complement to TSA and comment that:

> "if target situation analysis tries to establish what the learners are expected to be like at the end of the course, present situation analysis attempts to identify what they are like at the beginning of it."
>
> Songhori (2008:10).

The term "present situation analysis" was introduced by Richterich and Chancerel (1980) as cited in Songhori (2008:10) and treats learners themselves as the sources of information with reference to their present abilities.

Pedagogic Needs Analysis

The term proposed by West (1998) comprises three types of analysis: Deficiency Analysis, Strategy Analysis or Learning Needs Analysis and Means Analysis. Deficiency Analysis forms the basis of the language syllabus as it provides information to fill the gap between PSA and TSA by analyzing learners' deficiencies or lacks (Hutchinson & Waters, 1987).

Strategy Analysis or Learning Needs Analysis concentrates on the students' perceptions of their needs and endeavours to establish *how* learners wish to learn rather than *what* they need to learn. Hutchinson & Waters (1987) advocate for a framework for analysis of learning needs. The framework should comprise the following questions:

- Why are the learners taking the course?
- How do the learners learn?
- What resources are available?
- Who are the learners?
- Where will the ESP course take place?
- When will the ESP course take place?

Means Analysis investigates the environment in which the course will be run.

Songhori (2008:16) completes the picture of needs analysis with register, discourse and genre analyses, which were discussed in a greater detail in Chapter I of the present book.

Apart from the terms presented by Songori (2008), Jordan (1997:28) mentions language audits which are described as

> "large – scale exercises in defining language needs carried out for companies, regions and countries (…) which provide data and may suggest some educational policies to be implemented over a period of time".

A modern and comprehensive concept of needs analysis is provided by Dudley-Evans & St. John (1998:125), which encapsulates all the above mentioned approaches.

According to Jordan (1997:23), a needs analysis should commence with establishing the purpose of analysis and the student population. After that the approach(es) ought to be decided and limitations or constraints acknowledged. Subsequently, the methods of collecting data ought to be selected, the data itself collected and results then analyzed and interpreted. The next step is the implementation of decisions with reference to syllabus, content materials and methods. Finally, the procedures and results are evaluated.

As Bacha & Bahous (2008) underline, a needs analysis contributes to a great extent to effective ESP syllabus design, its development, implementation and assessment. Moreover, it helps to recognize what students need to study and what teachers need to teach, and at the same time presents the view of the user- institution. Nevertheless, some scholars question its objectivity and reliability.

2.1.2 Critical approach to Needs Analysis

There is a considerable amount of literature on the critical approach to needs analysis. Basturkmen (2006:19) presents an overview of the most problematic issues:

- needs analysis too often serves the interests of the institutions at the expense of learners (Benesch 1996),
- learners may not always be reliable sources of information on their own needs – especially if they are unfamiliar with the work they intend to perform or subject they are to study (Long,1996 as cited in Basturkmen 2006),
- objective needs may not match subjective needs – law students may objectively need to deal with, for example, contracts but may want to read texts in English on other general interest subjects,
- as Hutchinson & Waters (1987) remark, language needs are not necessarily learning needs – the fact that learners need to use certain language structures in their target environment does not mean that they will be ready to acquire them,
- learners with basic knowledge may not be aware or unable to describe these needs in any meaningful way,
- it is difficult to predict language use in specific situations and although ESP may produce a view of language needs (e.g. Munby's Communicative Needs Processor) it may fail to take into consideration the variation of language use that exists in any target situation,
- perspectives and perceptions of needs differ and are often in contradiction, thus the teachers (needs analysts) themselves have to decide whose perspectives and perceptions to take into account; therefore, the needs analysis cannot be considered a reliable tool (Brindley 1989; Benesch, 1996; Spratt, 1999),
- course designs based on needs analysis may lead to language training rather than language education, "learners are trained

to perform a restricted repertoire of the language rather than to develop underlying linguistic competence of language (Widdowson, 1983),

- it is often used to "get others to conform to established communicative practices" (Benesch, 2001),

2.1.3 Collecting data for needs analysis

Dudley – Evans & St. Johns (1998: 132) outline the main sources of data for needs analysis. They are:

- the students & ex-students,
- people working and studying in the domain,
- documents relevant to the field,
- clients,
- employers,
- colleagues,
- ESP research in the field.

The data for needs analysis may be collected by numerous means. An elaborate summary of the various techniques of data collection is provided by Jordan (1997:30-39). They are:

- advance documentation (about educational background, previous attended courses etc.),
- language tests at home,
- language test on entry,
- self-assessment (by means of questionnaires, forms or checklists),
- observation and monitoring,
- class progress tests (and error analysis),
- surveys (questionnaires),
- structured interview (comprises prepared questions to which the answers are noted and recorded; allows for follow-up questions),
- learner diaries (based on introspection, provide insights into students' learning experiences),
- case-studies (supply comprehensive information and insights, although may be time – consuming),
- final tests,
- evaluation / feedback (often in the form of questionnaires or round-up discussions),

- follow-up investigations (frequently in the form questionnaires or interviews),
- previous research.

All of the techniques contribute to gathering the data necessary to plan an ESP syllabus but it may be stated that questionnaires play a central role in the process. The advantages of conducting questionnaires and their role in the course planning, are not in doubt. As Davies (2006) remarks they may remind the learners that they are valued participants in the classroom, whose opinion may affect the shape of current and future courses. Moreover, they are a reliable, relevant and effective means in the particular context, prompting changes when necessary. Finally, they may diminish the level of learner misinterpretation of teacher intentions. (Kumaravadivelu, 1991; as cited in Davies 2006).

2.2 Selecting and grading content for ESP syllabus

As it has been stated above, selecting and grading content depends on balancing between different criteria to suit a particular context and circumstances. In the case of an ESP syllabus two more aspects need to be considered. The first is the question of the specificity of a course, the latter refers to the role of ESP syllabus components.

Narrow vs. wide angle course designs

It may be interesting to pose the question: "how specific (narrow-angled) should ESP courses be?" Even within the same field of study there might be learners with different needs. Some researchers (e.g. Dudley–Evans & St. John, 1998) opt for a narrow angled course in cases where needs are limited and as Basturkmen (2006:25) states " the course can legitimately focus on new target events and use content or topics from one discipline". Where needs are more general, the range of target events, content and topics will be wider. Other scientists refer to research results in estimating the specificity of the course. Basturkmen (2006) reports on the findings of Claphman (2001) and Ferris (2001). Claphman (2001) investigated the effect of background knowledge on reading comprehension in EAP. His research revealed that students differ widely in so far as their background knowledge is concerned – not necessary in terms of the specificity of texts they read. Ferris (2001), on the other hand, in his survey on designing ESOL academic writing classes in the USA showed that academic writing programs which focused on developing a set of generalized writing skills (with the expectation that the learners will transfer these general skills and strategies in writing tasks to their own specific discipline) were more popular than the programs which concentrated on teaching students the norms of the specific discipline. The above research seems to indicate that narrow- angle ESP courses are not always practical and feasible as learners can later transfer what they have learnt during a more general course to their own specific field of study.

ESP syllabus components

Some scholars (Jordan, 1997; Basturkmen, 2006) make a binary distinction between ESP syllabus components. Basturkmen (2006), for example, makes a distinction between **specific** and **specifiable elements** of the ESP syllabus. She claims that certain language forms or features (Language System) and skills (Language Skills) occur and are used more frequently than others, not necessarily only in the target specific environment. She calls them specifiable elements of the ESP syllabus. However Language Use and Content (i.e. conceptual and cultural items) are critical in the target environment and constitute specific elements in ESP design. Jordan (1997:73-75), on the other hand, distinguishes between EAP components and non-EAP components. On the basis of the surveys he conducted, he enlists numerous EAP components, the top three content areas being: general study skills, international issues, subject-specific language/topics. Non-EAP components i.e. grammar, vocabulary development, pronunciation, so-called “survival” English (e.g. greeting, ordering food, getting to places etc.) also play an important role in ESP courses as they serve as a necessary supplement to the main study skills, fulfill perceived present and future need and finally, provide useful variety.

***

A number of different syllabus types have been identified in the literature. Although some types of syllabus might be preferable for ESP courses (like e.g. task-based syllabuses) there are no restrictions as far as the type of syllabus is concerned. A syllabus designed for an ESP course does not have to practise and does not often practise all language skills equally - skills indispensable in a particular ESP course like business correspondence would seem to be completely irrelevant in General English courses. Therefore, as Komorowska (2006) remarks, a *skewed syllabus* which takes into consideration the criterion of usefulness and the criterion of learners’ needs would be much more successful in the learning and teaching process than a *balanced syllabus* where all language skills are taught proportionally.

What is critical, however, in ESP courses, as many scholars (Hutchinson & Waters, 1987; Komorowska; 2006, Rabbani, 2006) underline, is that: "the content should be derived through a process of consultation and negotiation with the learners, the consideration being the communicative needs of the learners" (Nunan, 1988:55). Therefore, a needs analysis is a central element in ESP syllabus (course) planning as it asks questions about learners' needs, the expectations of the user-institution along with the features of the actual teaching situation. However, some scholars question its objectivity and validity, claiming that it is a biased tool favouring the policies of the user-institutions, where objective needs are overemphasized at the cost of subjective needs.

There are also other constraints and variables that need to be taken into account in making decision about course design like, for example, budgets, time or available equipment and materials.

CHAPTER THREE

SELECTION AND EVALUATION OF MATERIALS FOR ESP

1. The development of ESP materials

1.1 The purpose of ESP materials

Dudley-Evans & St. John (1998) mention four reasons why materials are used in the ESP context. In the ESP classroom materials are exploited as a source of language, a learning support and for reference. In addition, they motivate and stimulate students. As Dudley-Evans & St. John (1998:170-171) comment, ideal ESP materials should:

- present real language,
- maximize exposure to the real language (as in some situations in the ESP classroom they may be almost the only source of English),
- be reliable and consistent,
- stimulate cognitive processes,
- be challenging,
- offer new ideas and information (taking into account learners' experience and knowledge),
- include input which could be used outside the learning environment,
- take into consideration learners' needs and learning strategies,
- be complete, well laid out and self-explanatory (to enable often busy ESP learners to study on their own).

1.2 Types of ESP materials

There is a wide selection of subjects covered by the term ESP and it is not feasible to decide on one type of ESP materials only. Four possible ways of materials application in ESP classes are mentioned in the literature

(Hutchinson and Waters, 1987; Barnard & Zemach, 2003; Bocanegra-Valle, 2010). These are:

- published course materials (also called textbooks),
- materials writing (refers to so called tailor-made or in-house materials),
- authentic materials,
- materials adaptation,

1.2.1 Published course materials

The roles and functions of course books are thoroughly presented by Rubdy (2003:38-41). She claims that published materials are invaluable in the class even though some scholars object to using them. The opponents state that they do not always provide the types of texts and activities that a teacher needs for a particular class, limit the freedom of the teacher, predetermine the content and procedures for learners and may serve a range of commercial interests of publishers. Robinson (1991:58-59), Bell & Gower (1998:117), El-Dahks (2011), Tomlinson (2012), on the other hand, enlist a number of benefits for the use of course books. These are:

- course books fulfil a wide range of practical needs (in different contexts),
- course books constitute a kind of route map where both teachers and learners can reflect on what has been done and what will be done, hence ensuring security and predictability which again prompt negotiation and exploration of the materials,
- thanks to course books, teachers can concentrate on other important aspects of lesson planning (like for example, adaptation of materials and supplementation),
- save time and money if compared to tailor-made materials,
- as published materials are often developed by experts in the field, they are frequently better designed and organised than teacher-written or learner-generated materials.

The use of published course materials for ESP classes similarly to course books for English for General Purposes implies advantages and disadvantages. The role, functions and evaluation of such materials do not differ, as Bocanegra-Valle (2010: 150) remarks in any language teaching/ learning "there is a need to examine the implications that certain materials may have for a particular course". What may be peculiar to the ESP area, however, is that hardly any single course book will be exploited from the beginning to the end due to the specificity of the subject-content. As

Barnard & Zemach (2003) comment, publishers are reluctant to publish materials which have a very limited specialist target group. Consequently, such materials have to be supplemented by in-house and/or adapted materials.

1.2.2 Materials writing

There are different views on the issue of the design and production of teacher-written materials. Some writers (Hutchinson & Waters, 1987; Sheldon, 1988; Robinson 1991) consider the whole process time–consuming, intensive and "best-regarded as the last resort, when other possibilities of providing materials have been exhausted" (Hutchinson & Waters, 1987). Conversely, other scholars (Block, 1991) believe that teachers should produce their own materials and for some part of the time replace the commercial course book with their own materials. In this way they can be sure that their materials appeal to students directly, they are up-to-date, relevant and involving. There are also some researchers (Dubin & Olshtain, 1986) who opt for team writing due to the shortage of time and complexity of tasks.

Barnard & Zemach (2003) pose the question: "what makes a good materials writer?" They comment that s/he should be a good teacher even though they add, that not all good teachers are prospective good materials writers. According to Barnard & Zemach, a good materials writer should possess:an acceptable linguistic knowledge,

- general teaching experience,
- experience of writing general English materials,
- an interest in the learning/teaching process,
- the ability to work with others,
- the ability to assess clarity and effectiveness of materials and respond appropriately,

and additionally, what may be useful in ESP teaching:

- teaching experience in the relevant specialism,
- some degree of knowledge of relevant specialism,
- and interest in the relevant specialism,
- familiarity with learning materials available for the specialism,

Barnard & Zemach (2003:313)

A selection of questions that may be helpful in materials writing is provided by Jordan (1997:262). The most crucial questions are:

- ✓ Why are the materials needed?
- ✓ Who are the students?
- ✓ Who are the teachers?
- ✓ What materials are needed?
- ✓ Where will the materials be used?
- ✓ When will the course be held?
- ✓ When is the material needed?
- ✓ When will it be produced?
- ✓ How are the materials to be produced?

Jordan (1997: 264) adds that there are a number of variables and constraints which need to be considered in materials writing. These are:

- the students' needs and learning objectives,
- the teachers' abilities, proficiency and self-confidence,
- the syllabus approach,
- the implemented methodology,
- the availability of resources,
- the time allocated,
- the amount of finance.

The variables and constraints listed above may result in numerous problems in materials writing. As Jordan (1997:269) points out, materials writing is quite a challenge owing to shortage of time (both for preparation and piloting), money (to finance additional teachers who help with writing), lack of co-operation from staff in specialist departments (in the case of ESP) and lack of self-confidence, experience and imagination on the part of the materials writer.

Contrary to the popular myth that every ESP teacher has to write his/her own materials, some researchers (Dudley-Evans & St. John, 1998; Barnard & Zemach,2003) state that only a small proportion of good teachers are also good designers of course materials. They claim that it is more pivotal that an ESP teacher is a good provider of materials by which Dudley-Evans & St. John (1998) mean being able to select from what is available, being creative with what is available, modifying activities to suit learners' needs and being able to supplement existing materials by providing extra input and activities.

Teacher-generated materials

As far as **teacher-generated materials** are concerned, according to Dudley-Evans & St. John (1998:176), the ESP teacher as materials designer and writer should possess the skills of matching carrier content to real content, providing variety, grading activity level to learning and language level, and presenting the material well.

Matching carrier content to real content is one of the most important elements of process for preparing new ESP materials (apart from selecting appropriate activities depending on available resources, group size, learning strategies and teaching approaches). It should precede drafting new activities and can be achieved in a twofold way, depending on the circumstances. If the teacher has some good input/carrier content, then s/he may determine what real content could be exploited, and finally where and how the real content matches the course framework. Another option for writing materials might be a situation where there is a gap in the course material and some materials are needed for meeting specific objectives. In this case, the ESP teacher needs to search for some suitable carrier content.

Variety is central in any language classroom, however, due to the specificity and complexity of ESP teaching/ learning it plays a critical role in preparing tailor-made materials thus making ESP materials motivating, stimulating and challenging. It can be understood as providing variety in teaching micro-skills and macro-skills, variety in activity types and in interaction. In this context it seems important to discuss the role of **case studies** as a perfect example of such activity types which not only integrates language and subject learning, but additionally introduces a lot of variety in the ESP class.

As Dudley-Evans & St. John (1998:192) emphasize the purpose of case studies is "to present students with some aspect of a real-life scenario, through which they can apply and integrate knowledge, skills, theory and any experience". Despite the fact that some drawbacks of using case studies have been noted (Dudley-Evans & St. John, 1998; Jackson, 1998; Tomlinson & Masuhara, 2003) such as the complexity of their texts and concepts, requiring a large amount of background reading, being quite time-consuming and difficulties with assessing the quality and quantity of students' performance, the advantages of implementing them into ESP course design are not in doubt. Case studies:

- are activity-based,

- often use authentic materials,
- involve the learners in both individual, pair and group work,
- foster a multi-skilled approach,
- enhance students' communicative, managerial, interpersonal, decision-making and problem-solving skills,
- view a dilemma from different perspectives,
- narrow the gap between theory and practice,

Jackson (1998:154); Dudley-Evans & St. John (1998:193)

Case studies can take the form of role-plays and simulations. In role-plays the learners perform the parts of different participants in a situation with assigned roles and arguments, whereas in simulations students are themselves put in problem-solving situations. Some scholars claim that simulations are even more useful than real-life tasks. Simulations, in their mind:

> "free the participants from the constraints which inhibited their thinking in their usual working environment and put them in situations which they have previously encountered (…) can create the optimum conditions for facilitating the sort of intake which can lead to useful and durable learning"
>
> Tomlinson & Masuhara (2003:462, 476)

The evidence presented above seems to indicate that case studies are an indispensable element of professional language courses in Medical English, Legal English or Business English.

Apart from matching carrier content to real content and providing variety, the writer of ESP materials needs to **grade exercises** (i.e. include tasks at different levels of difficulty and support learners in performing the tasks) and **present the material well** (i.e. in a consistent and attractive way).

Learner-generated materials

As Dudley-Evans & St. John (1998) remark, what makes ESP teaching different from EFL teaching is the content knowledge that ESP learners generally possess and need to use which the ESP teachers usually do not have. Some ESP teachers find the fact that they are not the "primary – knower" any longer, discouraging and uncomfortable. Others, however, perceive this as a perfect opportunity to involve the learners in the materials writing process. Learner-generated materials may include framework materials (a simple structure for use with any carrier content that is connected with learners' interests) or any other activities devised by learners themselves or authentic materials used by them in their professional domain. The proponents (Benesch, 2001; Sener, 2007) of learner-generated materials in the classroom emphasize their role in increasing students' motivation, improving their learning, and achieving lasting value outcomes. Nevertheless, they are generally exploited for very limited purposes (like assessment or grading) and limited disciplines (e.g. architecture or design) and thus they are rarely seen as a valuable component in most academic subjects.

1.2.3 Authentic materials

Authentic materials comprise written or audiovisual materials from the media like newspapers, magazines, radio, TV or the Internet, books, academic textbooks, documents used in a particular professional discipline or recorded live events like conferences, presentations or meetings. Undoubtedly, they are invaluable in the teaching/learning process (Vaiciuniene & Uzpaliene, 2010; Dastgoshadeh & Jalizadeh, 2011; Benavent, & Penamaria, 2011; Adam *et. al,* 2011; Lockwood, 2012). As Wong, Kwok & Choi (1995: 322) claim, "authentic materials can serve as a bridge between the classroom and outside world".

Additionally:

- they help to maintain students' motivation due to the fact that students learn the things that they really need (Gaffield-Vile, 1996; Peacock, 1997),
- they present the register and discourse, as well as semantic, lexical and syntactic elements specific for a particular field of study (MacDonald *et al.* 2000),
- they not only present specialized language, but also provide knowledge about a particular professional discipline (Gaffield-Vile, 1996),
- some language courses cover such rare or specialized domains that there are no textbooks or teaching materials available.

The motivational factor is one of the central justifications for the use of authentic texts for language learning. Peacock (1997:145) reports on his research on the effect authentic texts have on learners' motivation understood as: "adopted-learner interest, persistence, attention, action, and enjoyment". Peacock's research demonstrated, however, that the learners' motivation increased significantly, not because authentic materials are intrinsically more interesting and stimulating than materials designed specifically for language teaching/learning, as a number of scholars claim, but because learners who need the specialized language for professional purposes perceive them as relevant to the professional community to which they aspire.

Widdowson's (1978) dichtonomy between **"genuineness"** and **"authenticity"** may be considered a point of departure in attempts to define the **notion of authenticity**. He perceives genuineness as a characteristic of the passage itself and an absolute quality. In contrast, authenticity is a characteristic of the relationship between the passage and the reader, and its association with appropriate response (1978:80). He notes later that authenticity is not a quality of language, but it lies in the act of interpretation and is a type of response of the receiver (Widdowson 1979:165). Since then, five versions of "authenticity" have evolved. The original version of authenticity (later defined by Breen, 1985 as **text authenticity**) as MacDonald *et al.* (2000) remark:

> "attributes a pedagogical value to there being as close a match as possible between the language and social context of the input which learners receive in the classroom and the language and social of everyday life"
>
> MacDonald *et al.* (2000:253-254)

Breen's (1985:61-66) division seems to be the most elaborate and encapsulates four types of authenticity. These are:

- the authenticity of the texts which we may use as input data for our learners,
- the authenticity of the learners' own interpretation of such texts,
- the authenticity of the tasks conducive to language learning,
- the authenticity of the actual social situation of the language classroom.

Most scholars (Wilkins, 1976, Morrow, 1977; Hutchinson & Waters, 1987; Nunan, 1989; Peacock, 1997; Saraceni, 2003) agree that **authentic texts** are those real texts produced *by* native speakers *for* native speakers which are *not* designed for the purposes of language teaching. Guariento & Morley (2001) complete the definition with a comment that such a text is created to fulfill some social purpose in the language community in which it was produced.

The term **"learner authenticity"** refers to materials which involve the "learner's prior knowledge, interest and curiosity" (Breen, 1985:63). Some scholars (Taylor, 1994; Lee, 1995) opt for a binary distinction into **"text**

authenticity" and **"learner authenticity"** while defining the term "authenticity". Taylor (1994:4) emphasizes that:

> "authenticity is a function not only of the language but also of participants, the use to which language is put, the setting, the nature of the interaction and the interpretation the participants bring to both the setting and the activity".

He notes however, that this definition may be somewhat confusing as the classroom can also be seen as a real place. Lee (1995), on the other hand, makes a distinction between textually authentic materials (materials which are not written for teaching purposes but for a real-life communicative purpose) and learner-authentic materials (learner-centred materials which learners find motivating, interesting and useful). She stresses that some teachers believe that the goals and objectives of the course are achieved simply by providing students with authentic materials, but textually authentic materials are not essentially learner-authentic ones. She quotes Widdowson (1980) in that "authenticity can only be achieved when there is agreement between the material writer's intention and the learner's interpretation". Moreover, as she comments, learner authenticity not only refers to appropriate responses to the materials, but also to positive perceptions of them.

Task authenticity reflects the purpose to which language input is put. Guariento & Morley (2001) perceive "task authenticity" from a four -fold perspective:

- "authenticity" through a genuine purpose - the tasks are authentic if they prompt real communication and the language has been used for a genuine purpose,
- "authenticity" through real world targets – the tasks are authentic if they are relevant to real world needs,
- "authenticity" through classroom interaction – the tasks are authentic if their choice and position during the lesson are negotiated in the classroom (Breen 1985:67),

  'authenticity" through engagement – the tasks are authentic if the students are engaged by the tasks, and interested in the topic or their purposes.

Mishan (2005:75-83) provides a number of guidelines in order to design authentic tasks. In her opinion tasks are authentic if they:

- reflect the communicative purpose of the text on which they are based,
- are appropriate to the text on which they are based,
- elicit response to/engagement with the text on which they are based,
- approximate real-life tasks,
- activate learners' existing knowledge of the target language and culture,
- involve purposeful communication between learners.

Classroom authenticity refers to the question that the language teacher should consider i.e. "how to be authentic to the actual social situation" of the classroom (Breen, 1985: 66) whereas **teacher authenticity** pertains to the teacher's role with reference to authentic materials. As Thorp (1991) and Tudor (1993) cited in Lee (1995:325) underline, authentic materials cease being so if the teacher is not friendly, does not understand learners' needs and is not sensitive to them. It is the teacher as a leader and a central element who gives the teaching material its authenticity (Shomoossi & Ketabi, 2007:155).

1.2.4 Materials adaptation

There are abundant classroom situations when materials adaptation is required. Islam & Mares (2003:88) comment that they may pertain to methods (e.g. too mechanical exercises), language content (e.g. too much emphasis on grammar), subject matter (e.g. not involving topics), balance of skills (e.g. too much emphasis on reading), progression and grading (e.g. order of language items may need to be changed), cultural content (e.g. cultural references may need to be omitted) and image of materials (e.g. low quality of pictures).

McDonough & Shaw (1993) emphasize that adapting classroom materials may result in the personalizing, individualizing, localizing and modernizing of classroom materials. Islam & Mares (2003) add that on account of materials adaptation the language input is more accessible and engaging, higher-level cognitive skills and all sensory learning styles are exploited and finally learner autonomy is enhanced.

Useful techniques of materials adaptation are presented by McDonough & Shaw (1993) and Cunningsworth (1995). These techniques are:

- adding,
- deleting,
- simplifying,
- reordering,
- replacing material.

Adding means supplementing the existing materials and supplying more material. This can take the form of **extending** (i.e. the teacher provides more activities of the same type hence the change is in quantity) or **expanding** (i.e. the teacher adds something different to the materials thus it is a qualitative change). In the case of **deleting,** materials are amended either by **subtracting** (i.e. the teacher shortens the exercise, for example doing five sentences instead of ten) or **abridging** (i.e. the teacher changes the exercise qualitatively). **Simplifying** requires paraphrasing the instructions or the text to make it more accessible and manageable for learners and teachers whereas **reordering** means sequencing the activities in a diverse order if it is justified pedagogically. While **replacing materials** the teacher may decide to replace a whole activity or, a visual if s/he thinks that a different activity or a visual may serve the goals of the lesson better.

Darian (2001:2) remarks that "adapting original materials for language teaching is an incredibly subtle process – half art, half science" and provides a number of guidelines for materials adaptation referring to semantic, lexical, syntactic and discourse elements of the original text.

2. Selecting, implementing and evaluating materials for ESP classes

According to Dumitrescu (2000) while selecting the right materials, the ESP teacher needs to consider at least three basic aspects of the students' backgrounds:

- a linguistic background that affects classroom management, the choice, the arrangement and implementation of tasks during the lesson;
- a conceptual background that establishes the need for specificity or generality of information in the selected materials;
- a cultural background that influences student – teacher interaction, the formality or informality of classroom interaction, and the expectations of traditional instructor and student roles.

Dumitrescu (2000) mentions two more factors that are also crucial in the process i.e. **applicability** (by which she means that ESP materials are easier understood and perceived by students if their content matches their vocational interests and professional reality) and **adaptability** (by which she means the ease of the task design and the text manipulation which allows ESP materials to be effortlessly included in both oral and written communication courses). Barnard & Zemach (2003:317) draw attention to the fact that the process of ESP materials development and the roles of ESP of writers, learners and teachers are "inextricably interconnected" and one should not expect a "finished product" as the whole process is circular i.e. without a beginning or end. They, however, provide a model sequence for preparing ESP materials (figure 1) commenting that a number of steps can be omitted depending on the circumstances.

Step 1:
The needs and preferences of the students are determined by means of questionnaires and / or interviews

↓

Step 2:
The type of language contexts (e.g. lectures, business meetings) the course will focus on is decided

↓

Step 3:
The categories for presenting the language in the course (e.g. grammar, function, situation etc.) are decided on

↓

Step 4:
The language skills and sub-skills the course will focus on are established on the grounds of learners' needs and objectives

↓

Step 5:
The syllabus is designed

↓

Step 6:
The types of activities that will be used in the course are decided on

↓

Step 7:
The page layout of worksheets are chosen and templates are prepared

↓

Step 8:
The materials are prepared

↓

Step 9:
The materials are piloted and feedback is collected and collated

↓

Step 10:
The materials are revised

↓

Step 11:
The materials are used

↓

Step 12:
Students', teachers' and sponsors' feedback is collected during and after the course

↓

Step 13:
If necessary the materials are revised

↓

Step 14:

The course is reviewed cyclically

Figure 3-1. Barnard & Zemach's model sequence for preparing ESP materials

The issue of materials selection and evaluation is central to the successful teaching/learning process. Both selection and evaluation of materials relate to judging whether teaching materials serve a particular purpose. Following Rubdy's (2003:41) definition that:

> "... the selection of materials inevitably involves, or subsumes, a process of evaluation, evaluation can be undertaken for a variety of purposes and carried out in a variety of ways. In the selection of materials, on the other hand, what assumes primary importance is the analysis of learner needs and interests and how these are addressed. Consequently, in the selection of materials usually it is the most appropriate rather than the best that wins."

... it can be assumed that the term "evaluation" in this chapter may be used to refer to both selection and evaluation of materials.

Materials evaluation, as Tomlinson (2003:15) defines it, is " a procedure that involves measuring the value (or potential value) of a set of learning materials" in diverse contexts. It measures, for example, the flexibility, credibility, validity, and reliability of materials, along with their ability to interest and motivate the learners and the teachers and to fulfil administrative requirements.

2.1 The types of materials evaluation

Although, as Tomlinson (2003:23-33) remarks, it is possible to identify some principles of materials evaluation in general, they will not always relate to all types of evaluation. In his mind the most effective and reliable procedures are determined if the principles are applied to – "the contextual circumstances of the evaluation". Therefore, he advocates distinguishing three types of evaluation: pre-use evaluation, whilst-use evaluation, and post-use evaluation. In **pre-use evaluation** the potential value of the materials for their users is predicted. Tomlinson (2003) emphasizes that it is frequently quite subjective and impressionistic as it takes the form of a teacher browsing through a course book to assess its potential value. **Whilst-use evaluation** is more objective and reliable than pre-use evaluation (which relies on predictions) as it involves measuring the value of materials whilst using them or whilst observing them being used. It can relate to judging, for example, the clarity of instructions and layout, credibility, achievability and comprehensibility of tasks or practicality, teachability and flexibility of materials. Tomlinson (2003:24) emphasizes, however, that although it can assess short-term memory, "it cannot measure durable and effective learning because of the delayed effect of instruction". **Post-use evaluation** is considered the most valuable type of evaluation as it assesses the actual effects of the materials on the users. Moreover, it can measure both short-term and long-term outcomes of the use of the materials hence provides indispensable information about the further use, the adaption or amendments to the materials that have been exploited.

2.2 Evaluation models

In theory there are numerous evaluation models (Breen & Candlin, 1987; Sheldon, 1988; McDonough & Shaw, 1993; Cunningsworth, 1995; Jordan, 1997; Rubdy, 2003) that have been designed to help teachers to make a selection of teaching materials. They vary in the extent to which they reflect different priorities and constraints. A selection of some of them is presented below.

Breen & Candlin (1987:13) present their evaluation model in the form of a guide which is supposed "to assist teachers in choosing materials which will be most appropriate to their own learners at various levels and in various teaching settings". The guide is comprised of two phases. Phase One consists of questions which refer to the usefulness of materials, specifically with reference to the aims and content of the materials, the requirements towards learners and teachers, the functions of materials as a classroom resource. In Phase Two the questions are evaluated more closely and some criteria for the choice and use of materials are proposed. Breen & Candlin (1987) suggest their questionnaire as a starting point for appraisal.

McDonough & Shaw (1993), on the other hand, distinguish between "external evaluation" and "internal evaluation". The former means judging the materials from the outside (i.e. cover, introduction, contents page etc.) and the latter is based on four factors: the usability, the generalisability, the adaptability and the flexibility and pertains to a more detailed assessment.

Littlejohn's analysis (1998 as cited in Rubdy 2003) focuses on materials as a *pedagogic* device and refers to them from a two folded perspective. Materials are perceived either as a *publication* (i.e. physical aspects of the materials) or as a *design* which relates to the process of its production and use (i.e. aims, selection of tasks, language and content).

Rubdy (2003:45-54) proposes an evaluation framework based on three broad categories (psychological validity, pedagogical validity, process and content validity), each assessing the potential validity of materials. Psychological validity relates to the learners' needs, goals and pedagogical requirements. The following issues may be assessed within this category: rationale/learners' needs, the learners' independence, autonomy, self-development, creativity and co-operation. Teacher's skills, abilities, theories and beliefs fall under pedagogical validity. Process and content validity refers to "the methodology, content, format, layout and design features of the materials as well as theoretical assumptions about language and language learning that underpin them".

The evaluation checklists play a central role in the evaluation process, as they act as a facilitator in the process of materials selection. There are abundant proposals for evaluation checklists in the literature. A thorough review of forty eight checklists selected by writers in various publications in the period 1970-2007 is presented by Mukundan & Ahour (2010). The authors present the checklists in chronological order, paying attention to their qualitative and /or quantitative character along with the outline format. They also determine their length, the common criteria and their overall structures.

***

The development, selection and implementation of materials for most ESP courses requires not only considerable engagement and flexibility from the ESP teacher but also time. Due to the specificity of subject-matter specialisms in diverse courses, published materials may be insufficient and need to be supplemented or substituted by tailor-made or adapted materials. This may deter many teachers from taking on the challenge of ESP teaching, as they perceive the whole process as being too lengthy, too demanding and too complex to grasp. It can be stated, however, that the benefits that can be derived (e.g. enhancing students' language competence, achieving the course objectives and increasing motivation) definitely outnumber the drawbacks associated with the process.

CHAPTER FOUR

ASSESSING AND TESTING LANGUAGES FOR SPECIAL PURPOSES

1. Key issues in assessing and testing

1.1 Assessment vs. testing

Classroom assessment encapsulates a vast variety of options which can be divided into formative and summative assessment (Black *et al.,* 2003; Harmer, 2003; Garrison & Ehringhaus, 2007). **Formative assessment** is part of the instructional process and relates to the kind of feedback both teachers and learners receive in the ongoing teaching and learning context. It may help teachers to improve and refine their teaching and students advance their learning and performance. Formative assessment may encompass anecdotal records, quizzes and essays, diagnostic tests and lab reports. **Summative assessment** is "given periodically to determine at a particular point in time what students know and do not know (…) i.e. student learning relative to content standards" (Garrison & Ehringhaus, 2007:1). Summative assessment includes entrance and final exams, along with end-of-term or semester exams.

Dudley-Evans & St. John (1998:210), on the other hand, distinguish between **assessment** and **testing** stating that " assessment is a process of measuring, and one formal method of measuring is to test". From their perspective, assessment can include "less formal, more qualitative methods" conducted to provide feedback to aid learning, whereas tests serve as a comparable measure of competence.

1.2 Types and characteristics of tests

If we consider the reasons for testing, there are four main categories of tests presented in the literature (e.g. Jordan, 1997; Komorowska, 2005; Harmer, 2007). These are:

- **placement tests** which help to assess in which class/level prospective students should be placed; therefore they are concerned with the students' present ability and as the results are needed promptly, testing is performed without delay,
- **diagnostic tests** which serve to provide information about students' weak and strong points with the reference to particular vocabulary, grammatical structures and skills and to identify the areas of difficulties,
- **achievement tests** which refer to the materials included in the syllabus and course books and are designed to check whether the students have learned what they should have been taught,
- **proficiency tests** which are exploited to assess the suitability of students for specific courses such as at a foreign university or obtain some kind of certificate; they are not based upon particular syllabuses, books or teaching programmes but aim at providing general picture of a student's knowledge.

As far as characteristics of tests are concerned many researchers (Alderson *et al.*, 1995; Fulcher, 1997; Jordan, 1997; Dudley-Evans & St. John, 1998; Fulcher, 1999; Wu & Stansfield, 2001; Komorowska, 2002; McNamara & Roever, 2006; van der Walt & Steyn, 2008) follow Bachman & Palmer's (1996) framework of test qualities. They emphasize that the most pivotal quality of a test is its **usefulness** which is determined by six specific qualities i.e.:

- reliability,
- validity,
- authenticity,
- interactiveness,
- impact,
- practicality.

Reliability is described as consistency of test scores i.e. if the test is set to the same students on a different occasion and the results are the same providing that the students have not learnt anything more in the meantime, such a test is considered reliable.

Validity is perceived as " the appropriateness of a given test or any of its component parts as a measure of what it is purported to measure" Henning (1987:89). Validity is considered a complex concept (Alderson *et al.* 1995) and as Komorowska (2002: 23-25) claims, may be further divided into internal validity and external validity. **Internal validity** encompasses **content validity** (which relates to what is included in a test), **construct validity** (which refers to the "meaningfulness and appropriateness of the interpretations that we make on the basis of test scores" Bachman & Palmer, 1996:38) and **face validity** (which means the extent to which teachers and learners think the test measures what it is supposed to measure e.g. a suitable level of difficulty or appropriate content). **External validity** consists of **concurrent** and **predictive validity.** The former pertains to the comparison of test scores with some other measure exploited for the same students simultaneously to the test. The latter refers to the measurement of how well a test predicts future performance.

Authenticity is defined by Bachman & Palmer (1996:39) as "the degree correspondence of the characteristics of a given language test task to the characteristics of a target language use (TLU) task". For many scholars (Douglas, 2000; Lewkowicz, 2000; Wu & Stansfield, 2001; Tratnik, 2008;) it is a pivotal quality of language tests, as it provides a link between the TLU tasks and test performances and facilitates test takers' performance, due to the way in which they perceive the authenticity of test tasks.

Interactiveness means the degree and type of involvement of the test takers' individual characteristics in fulfilling a test task. By individual characteristics, Bachman & Palmer (1996:25) understand "the test taker's language ability (language knowledge and strategic competence, or metacognitive strategies), topical knowledge, and affective schemata".

Impact pertains to both the positive and negative influence that a test may have on different subjects. As Bachman & Palmer (1996) comment, this may be perceived from a two-fold perspective. At a micro level it affects the individuals themselves, whereas at a macro level it relates to the educational system and society. Some researchers (Dudley-Evans & St. John, 1998; Cheng, 2005) refer to the concept as a "**washback effect**" while others (Bachman & Palmer, 1996; McNamara, 2000; Shohamy, 2001) view the washback effect as a form of impact that tests may have. As Green (2007:2-3) remarks "while impact may occur at a *macro* or social and institutional level, washback occurs only at the *micro* level of the individual participants (primarily teachers and students)".

Practicality refers to " a range of issues, such as the cost of development and maintenance, test length, ease of marking, time required to administer the test, (…) ease of administration (…) and equipment required" (Dictionary of Language Testing, 1999). A practical test, in Komorowska's (2002:29) view, gives a detailed assessment without excessive effort, costs or time.

Even though all the qualities discussed above are equally important, as Weigle (2002:48) remarks, test developers should "determine an appropriate balance among the qualities for the specific situation" as it is not feasible to "maximize all of them".

2. Testing language for specific purposes (LSP)

As some researchers claim (Wu & Stansfield 2001:204) "the line between a LSP test and a test for general purposes is often blurred". They state that LSP testing is not at variance with other types of language tests as far as the qualities of good practice are concerned, as any good test (irrespective of the fact of whether it measures general or specific purpose language proficiency) should be reliable, valid, authentic and practical. However, some scholars, quoted by Douglas (2001:2) allege that specific purpose tests are frequently unreliable and invalid "since subject knowledge interferes with the measurement of language knowledge". Others remark that specific purpose language proficiency is nothing other than general purpose language proficiency with subject-specific vocabulary. In addition, for some researchers, specific purpose language testing lacks theoretical justification.

Other researchers (Douglas, 2000; Tratnik, 2008), however, strongly advocate the need for LSP testing for two main reasons. From their point of view, language performance varies with context and specific purpose language is precise. Douglas (2001:6-7) emphasizes that it is not sufficient to provide test takers with the task pertinent to the subject-matter specialism but "to engage the test taker in tasks which are authentically representative of that situation", that is, such tasks where "both language ability and knowledge of the field interact with the test content in a way which is similar to the target use situation". As far as the other reason for LSP testing is concerned (i.e. the precision of specific purpose language), it is held (Douglas, 2000; Tratnik, 2008) that each technical language, used in any professional discipline, has particular features which people who work in the discipline must manage. This is especially vibrant as far as Legal English is concerned. The specificity of legal language (discussed in Chapter I) serves precise communication among members of the legal profession.

There is a limited literature with reference to defining the concept of LSP testing. A comprehensive study on assessing languages for specific purposes was undertaken by Douglas (2000), who provided a precise definition of a specific purpose language test:

> "A specific purpose language test is one in which test content and methods are derived from an analysis of a specific purpose target language use situation, so that test tasks and content are authentically representative of tasks in the target situation, allowing for an interaction between the test taker's language ability and specific purpose content knowledge, on the one hand, and the test tasks on the other. Such a test allows us to make inferences about a test taker's capacity to use language in the specific purpose domain."
>
> Douglas (2000:19)

Responding to the criticisms with reference to the justification for LSP testing Douglas (2000) comments that **authenticity of task** and **the interaction between language knowledge and specific purpose knowledge** are the features which distinguish testing in LSP from more general purpose language testing.

2.1 Authenticity of task

The notion of authenticity and its types (i.e. text, task, learners' and classroom authenticity) has been discussed in Chapter III of the present publication with reference to selecting and developing materials for ESP classes. On the basis of Widdowson's and Breen's considerations, Lewkowicz (2000:45-46) raises two issues of concern relating to the authenticity of tasks in LSP testing. One pertains to the authenticity of test tasks perceived as " genuine input and focused on the need to use texts that had not been simplified and tasks that simulated those that test takers would be expected to perform in "the real world" outside the language classroom". Another concern refers to the question of whether or not authenticity of test tasks is central to all stakeholders in the testing process. As Lewkowicz (2000) remarks, Widdowson's distinction between genuine and authentic language, provoked the change to pre-communicative testing practices which started to focus on learners' abilities to use language in context rather than their knowledge about a language. From this perspective, authentic materials were an indispensable element of any test of communicative language ability, and hence preferable in the assessment of oral language and LSP testing. Such a propensity, as Lewkowicz (2000) points out, resulted in dichotomy between test texts where "authentic texts" (i.e. texts which had not been altered or simplified in any way) were considered more valuable in assessing LSP than "inauthentic texts" (i.e. prepared for pedagogical purposes) which were frequently perceived of as "inferior". Lewkowicz (2000) argues, however, that "this dichotomy proved unhelpful since it tended to ignore a number of salient features of real-life discourse". She emphasizes (following Selinger 1985) that not all native speakers understand all authentic texts as such texts also differ in complexity depending who they are targeted at and the amount of shared information between interlocutors. Additionally, extracting the text from authentic materials for testing purposes may make it "disauthentic", as according to Widdowson (1994: 386) authenticity is "non-transferable". Lewkowicz (2000) also notes that authentic test tasks (i.e. tasks which reflect real-life but are not actually so, even though they may be made to look like real-life tasks, do not have to give rise to genuine interaction. "Test takers need to cooperate and be willing to abide by the 'rules of the game' if simulations are to be successful in testing situations"(Spolsky 1985 after Lewkowicz 2000:47).

Bachman & Palmer (1996:49-50) propose a framework of task characteristics to determine the authenticity of test tasks. The framework is comprised of a set of features describing five aspects of tasks. The five aspects are:

- **setting** (i.e. physical setting, participants and time of task),
- **test rubric** (i.e. the structure of the test, instructions, the duration of the test, how the language that is exploited will be evaluated and scored),
- **input,**
- **expected response,**
- **relationship between input and response.**

Wu & Stansfield (2001:203) provide another model to ensure authenticity of test tasks in LSP testing. The verification of authenticity, in their mind, should be an ongoing process which relies on determining "the characteristics of the TLU" and making sure "that test tasks are as close as possible to tasks in real life which test-takers are expected to perform". Verification of this kind should be interactive i.e. practitioners (who serve as evaluators) and the test development team maintain "the communication channel". They also recommend the use of secondary resources in situations where primary resources are not obtainable.

Another concern raised by Lewkowicz (1997, 2000) is the question of whether authenticity matters for all the stakeholders of the testing process.

In her two studies, she researched individuals' (teachers' and learners') perception of authenticity. On the basis of the first study she concluded that neither native English-speaking nor non-native English-speaking teachers of EFL could distinguish between tasks that had been prepared especially for teaching purposes and authentic texts. In another study, students were to complete a questionnaire about their perceptions of two tests: an inauthentic test in the form of a multiple choice task and an authentic test in the form of an integrated test of listening, reading and writing. The results indicated that only very few students perceived the authenticity of the test as an important factor affecting their test performance. Taking into consideration the outcomes of the aforementioned research and bearing in mind the fact that there is little empirical research in this field Lewkowicz (2000) claims that the importance of authenticity and its indispensability in language tests can be challenged.

2.2 Language knowledge vs. specific purpose knowledge

Specific purpose knowledge also termed **background knowledge** understood as "prior familiarity with the content" (Krekeler 2006:100) is believed to have a facilitating effect on test performances. Numerous studies in this field (for example: Peretz & Shoham, 1990; Read, 1990; Jensen & Hansen, 1995; Gilakjani & Ahmadi, 2011) are however, open to doubt, due to the fact that in most of them the expected group of test-takers were not reported to achieve the highest scores on a given test (text or task). As Krekeler (2006:100) points out, this may result from the fact that:

- it is hard to establish a homogenous group with regard to previous knowledge and hence to measure the extent of their topical knowledge,
- textual qualities (such as the degree of specificity of a text, text readability, topic and genre), the type of questions, the level of proficiency of test takers affect the impact background knowledge may have on test performance.

An interesting study on the effects that background knowledge may have on test results was conducted by Claphman (1996). She studied test performance on reading modules of the International English Language Testing System (IELTS) – i.e. a test of academic English ability that, until its revision in 1985, contained reading sub-tests which related to moderately specific fields (like, for example, social sciences, humanities or physical sciences). The findings of her research were as follows:

- students achieved significantly higher scores on the reading sub-tests in their own subject area than on sub-tests outside their field,
- background knowledge in a subject specialism affected the test performance of postgraduate rather than that of undergraduate students,
- level of language knowledge i.e. the test takers' proficiency had an uneven impact on test performance – the relationships are presented in the table below.

Low language competence	Intermediate language competence	High language competence
Little effect of background knowledge on performance	Strong effect of background knowledge on performance	Little effect of background knowledge on performance

Table 4-1. Variable effects of background knowledge on reading test performance (as cited in Douglas 2000:32)

3. Public examinations in Legal English

Until 2002 there was no single examination that was used to verify language competence in the field of Legal English. In 2002 **the Test of Legal English Skills (TOLES)** appeared and four years after that, the **International Legal English Certificate (ILEC)** was introduced. Both exams resulted from the demands and expectations of law firms, corporations and institutions in relation to legal professionals that wanted to confirm their knowledge of Legal English. The introduction of the aforementioned examinations in Legal English was a milestone, not only in Legal English testing, but also with regard to Legal English teaching and learning, as it brought about an increase in the number of publications in this field (not only course books but also other teaching resources).

3.1 The Test of Legal English Skills (TOLES)

TOLES is the first international examination, created by a group of Legal English experts after years of consultations with legal practitioners. At the beginning, it comprised two levels: *TOLES Foundation* and *TOLES Advanced*. The division was somewhat confusing. First of all, the authors did not refer to any framework with regard to estimating the levels of competence. There were no placement tests provided – the mock examination was the only placement tool. Secondly, there was a huge gap between the levels: *TOLES Foundation* could represent the intermediate level and *TOLES Advanced,* the advanced level of English. In 2006 a new division was provided, taking into consideration the Common European Framework of Reference (CEFR), which, to a great extent, helped potential candidates to choose a level appropriate to their stage of learning. TOLES can now be taken at three levels:

- *TOLES Foundation* referring to A2-B1 levels (CEFR),
- *TOLES Higher* referring to B1-B2 levels (CEFR),
- *TOLES Advanced* referring to B2-C1 levels (CEFR).

All candidates receive a certificate. The certificate shows a candidate's score expressed as a percentage and an explanation of what that score means in terms of legal English skills.

The above mentioned levels of the TOLES examination do not cover the same format and content.

TOLES Foundation

According to the authors, *TOLES Foundation* is the examination aimed at candidates with a good command of English who are studying Legal English. The examination focuses on basic Legal English used in the appropriate context.

The authors declare that little or no knowledge of English law or American law is required during the *TOLES Foundation* examination, pointing out that the following aspects should be taken into consideration while preparing for this exam: passive knowledge of terminology and a sensitivity to use of register in the following general areas:

- fundamental vocabulary derived from specific areas of law like:
    - ✓ Contract law
    - ✓ Employment law
    - ✓ Business and company law
    - ✓ European Union law
    - ✓ Banking and finance
    - ✓ Intellectual Property law
    - ✓ The law of Tort

✓ Property law/real estate

- the vocabulary needed for candidates to compare the legal professions and systems of England and the USA with their own,
- the vocabulary essential to understanding written and oral contracts,
- an accurate use of prepositions in all areas of legal communication,
- a passive ability to identify mistakes common to non-native speakers,
- a demonstration of reading comprehension skills within a legal context,
- an active use of the accurate structure of simple sentences,
- an awareness of the formal style of written contracts.

Only two skills are tested: writing and reading. The TOLES authors believe that listening and speaking skills are more than adequately tested by general or business English exams. Grammar as such is not assessed, although of course grammatical accuracy within a legal context is required; however challenging grammatical structures are avoided. Use of the perfect tense, the passive and conditional sentences is very limited at this level.

The TOLES Foundation comprises different types of test exercises: error correction, gap filling, answering questions, multiple choice, matching, or cloze.

TOLES Higher

TOLES Higher verifies the candidate's skills that are appropriate at the intermediate level of learning legal English. It also focuses upon the language of written contracts and accurate letter writing. The authors state that similarly to the *TOLES Foundation,* the examination requires little or no knowledge of English law or American law although, as they remark, a basic awareness of the use of common law as opposed to a civil code would be useful. It is also emphasized here, that knowledge of law is not tested at any stage, but knowledge of legal vocabulary is fundamental. *TOLES Higher* specifically requires an active knowledge of, and a sensitivity to, use of register in the areas provided for in the *TOLES Foundation* and additionally in the field of prepositions and collocations in all areas of legal communication and modern letter writing. Apart from reading and writing, it includes listening in the context of specific vocabulary. Again, speaking is not tested.

Gap filling, multiple choice, open cloze, re-writing a letter (working on the appropriate register), answering questions, true/false questions are the prevailing test types. Grammar again, as such, is not assessed, although of course grammatical accuracy within a legal context is required.

Candidates' results for the *TOLES Foundation* and the *TOLES Higher* examinations are expressed as a percentage score; however there is no pass or fail mark.

The four bands are:

- 81-100: excellent
- 61-80: good
- 41-60: satisfactory
- 0-40: does not yet possess Legal English vocabulary.

TOLES Advanced

The examination tests the candidate's skills in using authentic Legal English, as required by international law firms. The examination evaluates the candidate's knowledge in the field of accurate and proper application of vocabulary, but also tests skills indispensable to every lawyer's work, such as letter writing or understanding and interpreting complex legal documents. As the authors again emphasize, candidates for the *TOLES Advanced* need little or no knowledge of English law or American law. The content of the test includes assessment of:

- knowledge of the specific legal vocabulary of the UK and US systems: areas of civil and commercial law, but as the authors point out, criminal terminology is not included. Most common vocabulary comes from, disciplines such as *inter alia*: the law of contract, business/commercial law, tort (the law of civil responsibility, suing for damages in case of accident, etc.), employment law, the law of intellectual property/copyright, taxation, basic insurance and banking terminology, international law,
- drafting and writing Legal English documents and letters, which involves an awareness of the unusual grammatical structure of legal English and the use of archaic terms and structures in general English as used by lawyers,

- the knowledge of the register of contractual documents; the candidates are required to provide a detailed analysis of an extract from a legal agreement to demonstrate their ability to understand and explain contractual documents,
- understanding spoken general English in a legal context, which requires a general awareness of the register used by lawyers in meetings/negotiations when using general English to discuss legal matters,
- the knowledge of collocations and prepositions used within a legal English framework.

Similarly to the *TOLES Foundation* examination, only two skills are tested: writing and reading. The TOLES authors believe that listening and speaking skills are more than adequately tested by general or business English exams or during job interviews at law firms. Grammar again, as such, is not assessed, although grammatical accuracy within a legal context is required.

Candidates are required to be able to deal with the following styles of question in the examination:

- complex texts within a legal context, including the explanation of short extracts from contracts,
- extracts from legal text books, legal documents (multiple choice or gap filling),
- redrafting from "legalese" into modern, plain English,
- transformation exercises testing knowledge of word families (verb, noun, adjective, etc., of the same root).

As far as the grading scale is concerned, six levels are displayed for the *TOLES Advanced* which start from a very low proficiency (GREEN 0-100) up to an advanced level of proficiency (GOLD 451-500).

GOLD	451-500	excellent
ORANGE	401-450	very good
RED	301-400	good
PURPLE	201-300	satisfactory
BLUE	101-200	almost satisfactory
GREEN	0 -100	basic

3.2 International Legal English Certificate (ILEC)

The examination was introduced in 2006 as the result of cooperation between Cambridge University Press and Translegal – a group of lawyer-linguists and from the start gained full recognition.
The ILEC aims at:

- evaluating candidates' skills in the international legal environment,
- confirming competences of the candidates for work while communicating with clients and co-workers,
- providing a positive and beneficial impact on the quality and content of Legal English courses,
- creating an examination, conducted according international standards, which will be fair with respect to all candidates,
- providing the possibility of comparing ILEC results with relevant qualifications.

Candidates can take the ILEC at two levels, which are referenced against the CEFR: B2 (corresponding to FCE - First Certificate Examination), and C1 (corresponding to CAE. (Certificate of Advanced English).

The ILEC authors emphasize that the ILEC does not test knowledge of law, but is aimed at assessing knowledge of Legal English. They focus on the following legal domains:

✓ Contracts,
✓ Employment law,
✓ Business associations,
✓ Corporate law,
✓ Real property,
✓ Remedies,
✓ Sale of goods,
✓ Debtor – creditor,
✓ Intellectual property,
✓ Competition,
✓ Negotiable instruments,
✓ Secured transactions,
✓ Environmental issues,
✓ Aspects of international law.

The authors point out however, that the list is not exhaustive and needs to be updated to meet the needs of its target users.

All four skills (reading, listening, writing, speaking) are tested at both levels.

The **reading** section consists of six parts (2500 words in total) and includes extracts from law textbooks and reference books, law journals, legal correspondence, reports and web pages. The texts focus on semantic precision, grammatical and lexico-grammatical knowledge, awareness of text structure, and understanding gist, detail, opinion and implication. Multiple – choice cloze, open cloze, word formation, multiple matching and gapped texts are the prevailing task types in the reading sections.

The **writing** section comprises two parts. The tasks focus on concise expression, a range of vocabulary and structure and grammatical accuracy. In the writing section candidates are required to write a letter and a memorandum.

There are four parts in the test of **listening** skills. The section focuses on understanding specific information, gist, main points and detail. Text types include presentations, lectures, announcements related to meetings, discussions, interviews and consultations. Multiple-choice questions, sentence completion and multiple matching are the main task types in the listening section.

The **speaking** section concentrates on exchanging personal and factual information, expressing and finding out about attitudes and opinions in the form of short exchanges with the interlocutor and between candidates and a three–way discussion. The Test of Speaking contains of four parts.

The band descriptors for the results of the ILEC examinations are as follows:

- Pass with Merit C1, advanced English (level CAE) - 80 - 100%
- Pass C1 advanced English (level CAE) - 70 - 79 %
- Pass B2 intermediate English (level FCE) - 50 - 69 %
- Narrow Fail - 45 - 49 %
- Fail - 0 - 44 %

3.3 TOLES and ILEC – similarities and differences

The two examinations share a number of common features; however the differences outnumber their similarities.

As far as the similarities are concerned:

- both TOLES and ILEC are designed for candidates of all subject specialisms within Legal English i.e. there are no separate sections for legal professionals who are, for example, Criminal Law or Civil Law specialists,
- all the questions are obligatory in the examinations,
- there is a preponderance of testing reading in both examinations.

In discussing disparities between the two tests it is necessary to note that:

- both TOLES and ILEC are referenced against different language levels: TOLES can be taken at A2-B1, B1-B2 or B2-C1 levels (CEFR) whereas ILEC can be taken at the B2-C1 level - the results obtained place the candidate at the appropriate level – at either the B2 or C1 level,
- TOLES and ILEC do not share the same grading scale: TOLES operates on band descriptors or the overall score given as a percentage, whereas the results for the ILEC are given only as a percentage of the scores,
- both examinations differ with regard to the extent to which technical vocabulary is tested; in TOLES (especially *TOLES Foundation*) there are some tasks which do not refer to subject specific vocabulary e.g. in one of the test tasks in TOLES *Foundation* the candidates have to decide on the appropriate preposition in the sentences which do not refer to a legal discipline at all e.g.:
  (A) Jenny works at New York City.
  (B) Jenny works in New York City. or
  (A) I will meet you on 25 July.
  (B) I will meet you at 25 July.
- The ILEC dominates over TOLES in the variety of test tasks and the number of skills tested; the ILEC tests all four skills (reading, writing, speaking and listening) while TOLES concentrates on reading and writing (*TOLES Foundation* and *TOLES Advanced*) or reading, listening and writing,
- although the creators of both examinations claim that neither the TOLES nor the ILEC test knowledge of the law or require background knowledge, a few inconsistencies are vibrant, especially in the ILEC examination e.g. the candidates are required to speak on topics where background knowledge of the discipline is indispensible, for example: "*the common legal issues*

involved in the sale of land" or "*the legal documents that are needed when a business is incorporated*".

***

Even though some scholars (for example Wu & Stansfield, 2001) challenge the idea of LSP testing, claiming that it does not differ from testing for general purposes, others (Douglas, 2000; Douglas 2001, Tratnik, 2008) strongly advocate the concept of LSP testing, stating that due to two of its main features (authenticity and interaction between language and background knowledge) LSP testing can be distinguished as a separate and distinctive part of a more general movement of English language testing. Furthermore, the impact (*backwash effect*) that the tests may have, cannot be ignored. The TOLES and ILEC are perfect examples of examinations, the introduction of which, has resulted in a significant increase in the number of publications in the field of Legal English and the amount of research carried out in this area, not only with reference to LSP testing, but also in relation to designing ESP syllabuses, or selecting and developing materials.

PART II

CHAPTER FIVE

A MODEL SYLLABUS FOR A COURSE OF ENGLISH FOR LEGAL PURPOSES

The syllabus presented in this chapter is a product of a two–cycle research programme conducted among 293 legal professionals (i.e. law students, lawyers, civil servants, or academic teachers) who were the target group for this research. The needs analysis conducted and the action research done helped to collect data with reference to the course content, teaching resources, methods and techniques to be included in the syllabus.

1. The course description

This model syllabus for a course of Legal English aims at developing learners' skills to communicate effectively in their profession, as well as expanding their Legal English vocabulary. The syllabus also targets improvement in a learner's autonomy, learning and communicative strategies. The course focuses on discussion and analysis of different areas of law as well as practising both receptive and productive skills.

The syllabus is designed for:

- teachers who teach Legal English both at universities and language courses,
- legal professionals (adult professionals involved in Legal English due to their work or study i.e. law students, lawyers, civil servants, or academic teachers).

The syllabus is comprised of 120 hours teaching hours in the whole educational cycle (e.g. two sessions of two academic hours per week for a year or one session of two academic hours per week for two years).

The syllabus may and should be adjusted to learners' specific needs. Modifications may refer to the course length, course content, methods, techniques and assessment procedures. It should, however, be noted that the syllabus ought to be expanded rather than shortened.

Legal professionals are learners who have already worked out their own system of studying - they know what their learning needs are and which learning strategies are the most effective for them. They also recognize the importance of Legal English for their profession and studies. Moreover, they are specialists in the content area and frequently contribute their professional knowledge and experience to the course content. Therefore, the teacher is no longer a "primary knower" (Dudley-Evans and St John, 1998) - participants are active partners in the learning process. The teacher's main role is to design the syllabus taking into consideration the learners' needs, to provide teaching resources but also to generate real, authentic communication in the classroom on the basis of students' knowledge.

2. The course objectives

The objectives of the course are as follows:

- to help learners achieve the necessary skills to communicate effectively with other people in their profession,
- to prepare learners to be able to react to new challenges connected with technological development, integration, globalization and exchange of information,
- to help learners understand the role of English in the contemporary world (business, science, politics),
- to help learners develop autonomy,
- to help learners expand their range of Legal English.

More specific objectives comprise:

- to help learners distinguish different registers and use them in an appropriate way,
- to manage formal correspondence,
- to understand authentic materials,
- to help the learners gain knowledge and skills necessary to pass examinations in Legal English.

3. The course content

The syllabus is divided into 10 thematic units. All four skills (speaking, writing, reading, listening) are practised in most of the units.

3.1 Vocabulary

The vocabulary section is dealt with according to the different needs of the group. It focuses on the following topics:

1. **Formal vocabulary vs. informal vocabulary (4h)**
- formal vocabulary vs. informal vocabulary,
- new meanings of well-known words in the context of Legal English e.g. *party, leave, produce*

2. **Basic concepts of Legal English (16h)**
- basic concepts and terms of Legal English
- sources of law in the UK, the USA, Poland
- systems of law in the UK, the USA, Poland (contrastive analysis)
- the Constitution as a source of law
- The court systems (the UK, the USA, Poland)
- Legal professionals

3. **Public International Law & European Law (12h)**
- Contemporary political systems
- International organizations (the EU, Council of Europe, UN, NATO)
- States
- International treaties and conventions
- Human rights

4. **Civil Law (18h)**
- Family law
- Inheritance law
- Intellectual Property law
- Property law
- Contracts and Torts (types of contracts and contract clauses, contract templates)
- Civil procedure

5. **Employment law (12h)**
- Types of jobs
- Applying for a job
- Types of employment contracts
- Termination of employment contracts

6. **Crimes & criminals (16h)**
- Types of crimes
- Types of punishments
- Trials
- Criminal procedure

7. **Financial & Tax law (12h)**
- Money & Banking
- Public Finances & Financial Institutions
- Taxes

8. **Company and commercial law (16h)**
- Types of business structures e.g. *sole trader, partnership etc.*
- Company formation and roles in company management
- Types of companies – American vs. British English
- The language of negotiating

9. **Administrative law & Administrative Procedure (6h)**
- Administrative law – basic terms
- Local government
- Administrative proceedings

10. **International examinations in Legal English (8h)**
- TOLES (Test of Legal English Skills)
- ILEC (International Legal English Certificate)

The thematic units and allocation of teaching time presented above is intended only as a suggestion. The course content with reference to particular legal areas and the allotted time should depend on the learners' needs and interests; thus it is necessary to conduct a needs analysis before embarking on a course. The order in which the particular thematic units are sequenced depends on the teacher; however, the thematic units *Formal vocabulary vs. informal vocabulary* and *Basic concepts of Legal English* introduce the learners to the specificity of Legal English, therefore it is advisable to include them at the beginning of the course.

Key vocabulary and concepts are used in context. Students are encouraged to utilise the vocabulary through the four skills, activities and work with authentic resources. The vocabulary section may also be enriched with material provided by the students (materials brought to class, glossaries may be prepared at the end of the section to share with other learners, and presentations given on the legal disciplines of particular interest to the participants).

3.2 The role of grammar

The grammar content is benchmarked against level B1 and B2 of CEFR. As the syllabus focuses mainly on developing the skills and vocabulary necessary to communicate in a relevant profession, it is recommended that grammar serves the role of "language check" rather than being explicitly taught during the course. The extent to which grammar is taught should, however, depend on the learners' needs and it is the teacher's role to decide on the proportion of time allocated to vocabulary and grammar. The range of grammar should include:

1. **Indicative (affirmative and negative) sentences and questions:**

- *present simple*
- *present continuous*
- *present perfect*
- *present perfect continuous*
- *past simple*
- *past continuous*
- *past perfect*
- *future simple*
- *future continuous*
- *future simple in the past*
- *future continuous in the past*
- *future perfect in the past (in conditional 3)*

2. **Modals**: *can, could, (be) able to, could have (done), must, can't, may, might, have to, must, mustn't, needn't, should, had better, it's time, would*
3. **Conditionals**: types: I, II, III; *wish*
4. **Passive voice +** *have/get something done*
5. **Reported Speech:** statements, questions and commands; verbs: *say*, *tell*, *ask*
6. **Imperatives & Exclamations**
7. **Questions and auxiliary verbs**: indirect questions, question tags
8. **Gerunds –*ing* and infinitives *to V***
9. ***used to V/ would V***
10. ***be/get used to Ving***
11. **Nouns:** countable, uncountable, singular / plural, collective nouns,
12. **Relative clauses:** defining, non-defining
13. **Articles**: *a, an, the*
14. **Adjectives:** comparison, adjectives ending in *-ed / -ing*
15. **Adverbs**
16. **Quantifiers**
17. **Numerals:** cardinal and ordinal numbers
18. **Pronouns & Determiners**
19. **Prepositions:** time, position, other uses
20. **Conjunctions**
21. **Expressing purpose, result and contrast**
22. **Language functions**
23. **Word order**
24. **Expressing reason, text organisers**
25. **Phrasal verbs and idioms**

3.3 Functions

Apart from the above objectives, the course aims at helping the target group to develop the following functions within particular skills, by requiring students to:

Writing

- fill in application forms of different types
- write instructions, reports, letters of complaint, notices, memos, CVs
- prepare projects
- draft contracts
- express their intentions, information in a quick, precise and grammatically accurate way
- use appropriate registers, layout, style, punctuation and spelling
- use self-correction

Listening

- gain an understanding of authentic materials: formal announcements, interviews, answer phones, news, TV or radio programmes, telephone conversations, commercials and reports to extent which enables them to grasp the main idea, a detail, the author's intentions, the type or function of the text
- understand other speakers
- distinguish different registers

Speaking

- hold conversations
- exchange information
- offer opinions (agree & disagree)
- negotiate, persuade and compromise
- solve problems
- interpret and summarise authentic texts

Reading

- develop their understanding of authentic material without using a dictionary to grasp main idea of the text (skimming) or to find a particular detail (scanning)
- improve and revise Legal English vocabulary on the basis of authentic material
- distinguish different registers

3.4 A sample section

The following is an example of the thematic unit on Employment Law with exercises for improving skills and expanding vocabulary in this area.

	Employment law	**Vocabulary:** • Types of jobs • Applying for a job • Types of employment contracts • Accident at work/occupational disease **Reading:** • *Job advertisements* – vocabulary work on authentic materials • *Employment agreements* – vocabulary work on authentic materials (the UK and the USA) **Writing:** • CV & application letter • Polish employment agreement – guided translation on the basis of American and English employment agreements **Listening:** • *Tips for a successful interview* – understanding main points **Speaking:** • Types of jobs / The question of unemployment /Harassment at work – pair work - agreeing and disagreeing • The need for HRM – role play **Integrated skills** (reading, speaking, listening): • jigsaw reading – Info for foreigners in Poland– *Terms of employment* **Speaking & Writing:** • *Accident at work*/role play, preparing an accident report

Table 5-1. A sample section on Employment Law

4. The course implementation

4.1 The rationale

The syllabus does not recommend one method but a mixed approach is used in designing and implementing a syllabus for a course of Legal English to meet learners' needs and interests. Three areas are considered with regard to a rationale for the syllabus: the learning environment, the role of the teacher and the activities exploited to achieve the course objectives.

The author believes that a supportive and positive environment is an indispensable condition to acquire knowledge and gain the necessary skills to communicate effectively with other people in their profession. As learners are a target group of adults with developed learning needs the teacher's role is to create such a learning environment which would enhance the process of learning. As a result, the learners' personal development and autonomy will improve and their confidence will increase. The role of the ESP teacher is, however, more complex and more responsible than teaching General English. The ESP teacher is more than a teacher, rather s/he is a "practitioner" (Dudley-Evans & St. John, 1998) who apart from teaching, provides materials, designs a syllabus, collaborates with subject specialists, conducts research and evaluates the course and the learners. The teacher's role is also to organize the class: to be aware of the class objectives, to have a good understanding of the course content, as well as to be flexible and willing to cooperate with learners and have at least some interest in the disciplines s/he is teaching. The flexibility is a key feature here. Legal professionals are not a homogenous group – they are law students and lawyers with different specializations (legal advisers, prosecutors, judges or civil servants) - even in the field of Legal English, there are specialists whose interests would not match. Therefore, it is essential, apart from the placement test (which evaluates the learners' command of Legal English), to conduct a needs analysis which would help to establish the prospective group's needs and expectations with reference to their Legal English course. Furthermore, it is recommended that the same needs analysis should be carried out during the course as research has revealed that what learners actually need is not always what they expected or believed they needed prior to embarking on a course. Moreover, the evaluation of the course should be on-going: whilst the course is being taught, at the end of the course, and after the course has finished. Both a needs analysis and post-course questionnaire is helpful in adjusting the course content, methods, materials to students' professional needs and interests. This might be particularly informative in situations such as the ones summarised below:

- to help students with a lower level of English during individual work at home,
- to compensate the extent to which a particular discipline is taught (if the learners feel that the time devoted to it was insufficient),
- to provide students with a higher level of English with some extra or more specialized materials to work with in or outside the class,
- to organize other forms of activities such as presentations or projects

4.2 Groupings

Learners' needs, their learning strategies, task types and conditions of work – all affect the choice of group size for a particular activity. Moreover, a diversity of work methods should be implemented in and outside the class. The following work groups for activities are suggested:

- whole class work,
- working in groups,
- working in pairs,
- working individually.

4.3 Techniques

Different techniques are recommended to practise the necessary skills to communicate effectively within the learners' profession.

Listening

It is advisable that the texts used for listening practise are, if possible, based on authentic materials (or adaptations of these to suit the learners' level). These could be:

- radio recordings,
- TV programmes,
- songs,
- interviews,
- formal announcements,
- telephone calls,
- lectures,
- presentations,
- negotiations,

- conferences.

The techniques used to advance listening skills comprise:

- listening for gist,
- listening for specific details,
- gap filling,
- multiple choice,
- dictations,
- putting things in the right order.

The example could be a gap-filling exercise on the basis of Barack Obama Nobel Lecture given in 2009 (Sierocka, 2011:39-40).

Task 2. Listen to Barack Obama Nobel Lecture (2009) and complete the gaps. The first letter is given to help you.

A Just and Lasting Peace

(1) Your Majesties, Your Royal Highnesses, Distinguished Members of the Norwegian Nobel Committee, citizens of America, and citizens of the world:

(2) I receive this honor with deep gratitude and great humility. It is 1) an a______ that speaks to our highest aspirations – that for all the cruelty and hardship of our world, we are not mere prisoners of fate. Our actions matter, and can bend history in the direction of 2) j______.

(3) And yet I would be remiss if I did not acknowledge the considerable controversy that your generous decision has generated. In part, this is because I am at the beginning, and not the end, of my labors on the world stage. Compared to some of the giants of history who have received this prize – Schweitzer and King; Marshall and Mandela – my accomplishments are slight. And then there are the men and women around the world who have been jailed and beaten in the pursuit of justice; those who toil in 3) h______ organizations to relieve suffering; the unrecognized millions whose quiet acts of 4) c______ and compassion inspire even the most hardened of cynics. I cannot argue with those who find these men and women – some known, some obscure to all but those they help – to be far more deserving of this honor than I.

(4) But perhaps the most profound issue surrounding my receipt of this prize is the fact that I am the Commander-in-Chief of 5) a n______ in the midst of two wars. One of these wars is winding down. The other is a conflict that America did not seek; one in which we are joined by forty three other countries – including Norway – in an effort to defend ourselves and all nations from further 6) a______.

(5) Still, we are at war, and I am responsible for the deployment of thousands of young Americans to battle in a distant land. Some will kill. Some will be killed. And so I come here with an acute sense of the cost of armed conflict – filled with difficult questions about the relationship between war and 7) p______, and our effort to replace one with the other.

(6) These questions are not new. War, in one form or another, appeared with the first man. At the dawn of history, its morality was not questioned; it was simply a fact, like drought or disease – the manner in which tribes and then civilizations sought power and settled their differences.

(7) Over time, as codes of law sought to control 8) v______ within groups, so did philosophers, clerics, and statesmen seek to regulate the destructive power of war. The concept of a "just war" emerged, suggesting that war is justified only when it meets certain preconditions: if it is waged as a last resort or in self-defense; if the forced used is proportional, and if, whenever possible, civilians are spared from violence.

(8) For most of history, this concept of 9) j______ war was rarely observed. The capacity of human beings to think up new ways to kill one another proved inexhaustible, as did our capacity to exempt from mercy those who look different or pray to a different God. Wars between armies gave way to wars between nations – total wars in which the distinction between combatant and civilian became blurred. In the span of thirty years, such carnage would twice engulf this continent. And while it is hard to conceive of a cause more just than the defeat of the Third Reich and the Axis 10) p______, World War II was a conflict in which the total number of civilians who died exceeded the number of soldiers who perished.

(9) In the wake of such 11) d______, and with the advent of the nuclear age, it became clear to victor and vanquished alike that the world needed institutions to prevent another World War. And so, a quarter century after the United States Senate rejected the League of Nations – an idea for

which Woodrow Wilson received this Prize – America led the world in constructing an architecture to keep the peace: a Marshall Plan and a United Nations, mechanisms to govern the waging of war, treaties to protect human rights, prevent genocide, and restrict the most dangerous 12) w______.

(10) In many ways, these efforts succeeded. Yes, terrible 13) w______ have been fought, and atrocities committed. But there has been no Third World War. The Cold War ended with jubilant crowds dismantling a wall. Commerce has stitched much of the world together. Billions have been lifted from 14) p______. The ideals of liberty, self-determination, equality and the rule of law have haltingly advanced. We are the heirs of the fortitude and foresight of 15) g______ past, and it is a legacy for which my own country is rightfully proud.

Speaking

Tasks chosen to enhance speaking should reflect real-life situations, covering the aspects which match the learners' needs, interests and experiences. The techniques used to improve speaking include:

- dialogues,
- describing pictures,
- dictation,
- role plays and simulations,
- discussions,
- games,
- presentations,
- expressing opinions,
- information gap.

Provocative statements (like in the example below) frequently generate a heated discussion.

Look at the sentences below. Mark them in the following way:
✓If you agree
x If you disagree
? If you partly agree and partly disagree

1. *Homosexual couples should not be allowed to adopt children.*
2. *Adopted children should have a right to know who their birth parents are.*
3. *Online adoption services (online services helping pregnant women find families who would adopt their baby) are a great idea.*
4. *Mothers look after children much better than fathers, so in case of divorce, children should always stay with the mother.*
5. *Getting a divorce should be made more difficult (e.g. a couple who want to divorce must take part in compulsory counselling for six months before a decision is taken)*
6. *The child should decide if s/he wants to live with either the mother or the father.*

Sierocka (2011:76)

Role plays and simulations as one shown below are very stimulating and motivating to speak.

Task 1. Work in three groups: A, B and C. Prepare your role and then take decisions about the prospects of further cooperation.

PROBLEM !!! A DIFFICULT PARTNER

Background

In 2009 Robert Zaradny with two other colleagues: Adam Marudny and Kacper Lojalny set up a professional partnership called "Zaradny and partners – Medical professional partnership". At the beginning everything went well but for the last six months things have been getting worse and worse. The Articles of Association of their professional partnership do not restrict the right of representation of the partnership, therefore all partners may conclude contracts on the partnership's behalf. Unfortunately, Robert Zaradny has concluded a number of unfavourable contracts recently - the level of antagonism among the partners has increased considerably and the atmosphere in the partnership is unbearable. The partners are meeting today to discuss the prospects of further cooperation.

Group A

You are Adam Marudny. You want to expel Robert Zaradny from the partnership. Although Robert set up the partnership, and at the start was its "driving force", his latest actions and the contracts concluded by him put the partnership in jeopardy. Apart from that, he is always late for meetings, hardly ever remembers to pay the employees but is forever demanding more money for himself.

Group B

You are Robert Zaradny. You have invested a lot of time and money in setting up this partnership. You have ideas, visions and connections. You think your partners (especially Adam Marudny) are not fair and they do not appreciate your work. Adam is always complaining. What is more, he has no idea how to solve problems and is not creative at all. You think he should leave the partnership. It is true that his contribution to the partnership was significant, but money is not everything! Moreover, any unfavourable contracts can still be annulled.

Group C

You are Kacper Lojalny. Actually you are between a rock and a hard place. You agree with Adam that Robert has been acting carelessly recently and that you might have problems with these unfavourable contracts. On the other hand, Robert is your best friend and you owe him a great deal.

Sierocka (2011:270)

Reading

Emphasis on exploiting authentic materials (or adaptations of these) should also be placed on practising reading. The types of texts encompass:

- newspapers,
- magazines,
- letters,
- official documents,
- templates,
- reports,

- novels,
- short stories,
- the Internet,
- leaflets,
- formal correspondence,
- academic publications,
- law publications.

The following techniques might be used to improve reading:

- understanding main points and expressions,
- understanding details,
- gap filling,
- answering questions,
- matching,
- cloze,
- multiple choice exercises,
- putting things in the right order,
- searching for particular information,
- jigsaw reading.

The following is an example of exploiting authentic materials for reading purposes.

Task 1. Match the headings given below with the appropriate article of the Charter of Fundamental Rights of the European Union. There are some extra headings.

- *Freedom to choose an occupation and right to engage in work*
- *Freedom of expression and information*
- *Freedom of assembly and of association*
- *Freedom to conduct a business*
- *Right to property*
- *Right to asylum*
- *Freedom of the arts and sciences*
- *Right to life*
- *Right to the integrity of the person*
- *Prohibition of torture and inhuman or degrading treatment or punishment*
- *Prohibition of slavery and forced labour*
- *Protection of personal data*
- *Right to marry and right to found a family*

- *Human dignity*
- *Right to liberty and security*
- *Respect for private and family life*
- *Freedom of thought, conscience and religion*
- *Right to education*
- *Protection in the event of removal, expulsion or extradition*

CHARTER OF FUNDAMENTAL RIGHTS OF THE EUROPEAN UNION

The Union therefore recognises the rights, freedoms and principles set out hereafter.

C 303/2 EN Official Journal of the European Union 14.12.2007

Article 2

1. Everyone has the right to life.

2. No one shall be condemned to the death penalty, or executed.

Article 3

1. Everyone has the right to respect for his or her physical and mental integrity.

2. In the fields of medicine and biology, the following must be respected in particular:

(a) the free and informed consent of the person concerned, according to the procedures laid down by law;

(b) the prohibition of eugenic practices, in particular those aiming at the selection of persons;

(c) the prohibition on making the human body and its parts as such a source of financial gain;

(d) the prohibition of the reproductive cloning of human beings.

Article 8

1. Everyone has the right to the protection of personal data concerning him or her.

2. Such data must be processed fairly for specified purposes and on the basis of the consent of the person concerned or some other legitimate basis laid down by law. Everyone has the right of access to data which has been collected concerning him or her, and the right to have it rectified.

3. Compliance with these rules shall be subject to control by an independent authority.

Article 10

1. Everyone has the right to freedom of thought, conscience and religion. This right includes freedom to change religion or belief and freedom, either alone or in community with others and in public or in private, to manifest religion or belief, in worship, teaching, practice and observance.

2. The right to conscientious objection is recognised, in accordance with the national laws governing the exercise of this right.

Article 12

1. Everyone has the right to freedom of peaceful assembly and to freedom of association at all levels, in particular in political, trade union and civic matters, which implies the right of everyone to form and to join trade unions for the protection of his or her interests.

2. Political parties at Union level contribute to expressing the political will of the citizens of the Union.

Article 14

1. Everyone has the right to education and to have access to vocational and continuing training.

2. This right includes the possibility to receive free compulsory education.

3. The freedom to found educational establishments with due respect for democratic principles and the right of parents to ensure the education and teaching of their children in conformity with their religious, philosophical and pedagogical convictions shall be respected, in accordance with the national laws governing the exercise of such freedom and right.

Article 15

1. Everyone has the right to engage in work and to pursue a freely chosen or accepted occupation.

2. Every citizen of the Union has the freedom to seek employment, to work, to exercise the right of establishment and to provide services in any Member State.

3. Nationals of third countries who are authorised to work in the territories of the Member States are entitled to working conditions equivalent to those of citizens of the Union.

Article 17

1. Everyone has the right to own, use, dispose of and bequeath his or her lawfully acquired possessions. No one may be deprived of his or her possessions, except in the public interest and in the cases and under the conditions provided for by law, subject to fair compensation being paid in good time for their loss. The use of property may be regulated by law in so far as is necessary for the general interest.

2. Intellectual property shall be protected.

Article 18

The right to asylum shall be guaranteed with due respect for the rules of the Geneva Convention of 28 July 1951 and the Protocol of 31 January 1967 relating to the status of refugees and in accordance with the Treaty on European Union and the Treaty on the Functioning of the European Union (hereinafter referred to as 'the Treaties').

Article 19
1. Collective expulsions are prohibited.
2. No one may be removed, expelled or extradited to a State where there is a serious risk that he or she would be subjected to the death penalty, torture or other inhuman or degrading treatment or punishment.

Task 2. Read the articles above again and find the words which mean:
a) agreement, approval (n.) -
b) obligatory (adj.) -
c) proceeding (n.) -
d) capital punishment (n.) -
e) ban (n.) -
f) professional (adj.) -
g) citizen (n.) -
h) to dispose of (property, esp. personal property) by will -
i) the act of forcing out someone or something (n.) -
j) place offering protection and safety (n.) -

Sierocka (2011:56-58)

Writing
It is rational to place writing tasks in a context that the learner is familiar with, which will facilitate the task performance and make it absorbing and thought provoking. The recommended techniques are as follows:

- self-correction,
- work on a model text (gap filling, choosing the correct version),
- peer correction,
- guided writing,
- sentence completion,
- planning pieces of writing (e.g. brainstorming).

The example provided below combines different writing techniques.

Task 1. Read the letter of complaint given below. Why is it inappropriate?

HOW NOT TO WRITE A LETTER OF COMPLAINT
My name is Jan Nowak,my transaction - ***Transaction Nr.: mT872q8mJudXF, Price: 48.00 euro,*** *(2009-11-03 12:03:25), Payment method: Creditcard,* ***Transfer from Charleroi Airport*** *to: Brussels private address - 1324 Av. Blue (211). Date: 2007. 12. 24 (WAW - W6 421 - Warsaw, Passanger: 5)*
There was no minibus at the airport!!!!!!
After we were waiting for one hour, with two small children, we had to take a taxi to Brussels !! (It was evening and day before Christmas)!! I tried to contact with you, but there was nobody on the phone given by you, in case of emergency !! And nobody from you tried to contact with me!!!!
Please send me back my money - 48 euro and the cost of taxi to Brussels - 100 euro, immediately!!!
Jan Nowak
I also send an information to wizzair - not to write about You as a comfortable and quick way to get to Brussels, because its not true!!
Please answer , otherwise I will write to the hungarian and polish police!

Task 2. Rewrite the letter so it has an appropriate layout, content and style (go to page 325 to see a model letter).

Sierocka (2011:124)

It is crucial to establish that the best results are achieved when tasks are organised in such a way that all practised skills are integrated to reflect real-life situations and to prompt active communication. Jigsaw reading exercises, working on projects, presentations, or posters as well as participating in lectures conducted in English (as within the Socrates Erasmus Programme) are examples of these types of activities.

4.4 Teaching vocabulary

Teaching specialised vocabulary is one of main objectives of a model syllabus for a course of Legal English. By this it is meant:

- understanding specialised vocabulary,
- learning specialised vocabulary,
- appropriate use of words and expressions in context,
- revising and expanding vocabulary of particular legal areas,
- preparing to solve examination tasks.

With regard to teaching specialised vocabulary, it is central to use authentic materials (or adaptations of these to suit the learners' level). They are of great motivational value – in class students learn vocabulary from primary sources, they are provided with resources which they may use in work or for their studies, they can simulate real, everyday situations in class. As a result, their confidence increases and personal development is enhanced. The following types of tasks may be used to introduce new vocabulary:

- providing an equivalent in the learner's native language,
- providing synonyms or definitions to present a new word or expression,
- presenting new words and phrases in context,
- using visuals or recordings.

The teacher's role (on the basis of a needs analysis conducted before the course) is also to suggest techniques which will facilitate the process of learning and expanding new vocabulary. These might include:

- taking down new words and phrases,
- preparing posters with new words and phrases,
- recording new words and phrases,
- frequent repetitions of new words and phrases aloud,
- making sentences or stories with new words and phrases,
- grouping news words and phrases (e.g. trees, thematic maps), (see example A below)
- word formation,
- multiple choice, (see example B below)
- gap filling,
- error correction (see example C below).

Example A:

Task 4. Complete the chart with the words:

borrower	*claimant*	*deceased*
defendant	*heir*	*immovable property*
offer	*landlord*	*lender*
licence	*loan agreement*	*mediation*
patent holder	*premarital agreement*	*separation*
spouse	*succession*	*tenant*
tenancy agreement	*trademark*	*will* *writ*

AREAS OF CIVIL LAW	***PEOPLE***	***CONCEPTS***	***DOCUMENTS***
Civil Procedure	__________, __________	__________	__________
Contracts	__________, __________	__________	__________
Family Law	__________	__________	__________
Inheritance Law	__________, __________	__________	__________
Intellectual Property Law	__________	__________	__________
Real Property Law	__________, __________	__________	__________

Sierocka (2011:69)

Example B:

Task 3. Read the articles below and choose the correct meaning of the words in bold:

1. authority
a) an expert *b) evidence or testimony* *c) e.g. the government*

2. observance
a) respecting *b) watching* *c) celebrating*

3. exercise
a) perform *b) practise* *c) do sports*

4.personality
a) character *b) identity* *c) a well-known person*

5. court
a) an area where games are played
b) a place where trials take place and legal cases are decided

c) the place of residence of a king

Article 126

(1) The President of the Republic of Poland shall be the supreme representative of the Republic of Poland and the guarantor of the continuity of State ***authority****.*
(2) The President of the Republic shall ensure ***observance*** *of the Constitution, safeguard the sovereignty and security of the State as well as the inviolability and integrity of its territory.*
(3) The President shall ***exercise*** *his duties within the scope of and in accordance with the principles specified in the Constitution and statutes.*

Article 165

(1) Units of local self-government shall possess legal ***personality****. They shall have rights of ownership and other property rights.*
(2) The self-governing nature of units of local self-government shall be protected by the ***courts****.*

Sierocka (2011:248)

Example C:
Correct five grammatical mistakes in the extract below.

Sub-section 1. Mediation

Art. 183^{1}. *§ 1. Mediation is voluntary.*
§ 2. Mediation procedure is set in motion based on a mediation contract or courts decision referring a case to mediation. A mediation contract may also be conclude by the expression of consent for mediation by the party if another party submitted a motion mentioned in Art. 183^{6}.
§ 3. A mediation contract determines in particular the subject of mediation, a mediators or a way of choose a mediator.
§ 4. Mediation take place before the institution of the proceedings, but if the parties agree to go to mediation, mediation can take place also in the course of proceedings.

Sierocka (2011:154)

4.5 Teaching resources

Course books:

- *Legal English – Niezbędnik przyszłego prawnika* by H.Sierocka (Publikator)
- *The Lawyer's English Coursebook* TOLES by C. Mason & R. Atkins (Global Legal English Ltd)
- *Business Law* by T. Smith (Pearson Education Limited)
- *International Legal English* by A. Krois-Lindner and Translegal (CUP)

Reference and supplementary materials:

- *Test your Professional English LAW* by N. Brieger (Penguin English)
- *Professional English in Use* by G. D. Brown & S. Rice (CUP)
- *Legal English* by W. R. Mckay & H. E. Charlton (Longman)
- *English for Polish Lawyers* by G. Błaszczyk and V. Ptasińska (Wydawnictwo Zrzeszenia Prawników Polskich)
- *Practical English for Lawyers* by A. Konieczna-Purchała (Beck)
- *Legal English* by M. Jakubaszek (Beck)
- *Lexicon of Legal Terms* by E. Myrczek (Beck)
- *Business English Readings* by P. Mamet (ed.) (Beck)
- *Tests in English Thematic vocabulary* by M. Misztal (WSiP)
- *Advanced Vocabulary & Idiom* by B.J. Thomas (Longman)
- *Intelligent Business Coursebook Upper-intermediate* by T. Trappe and G. Tullis (Pearson Education Limited)
- *English File Upper-intermediate* by C. Oxenden and Ch. Latham – Koenig (OUP)
- *Discussions A-Z Advanced* by A. Wallwork (CUP)
- *Cambridge Business English Activities* by J. Cordell (CUP)
- *Business Roles 2* by J. Crowther- Alwyn (CUP)
- *Clockwise Upper-intermediate* by H. Donaghue and H. Potten (OUP)
- *Oxford Handbook of Legal Correspondence* by R. Haigh (OUP)
- *Taboos and Issues* by R. MacAndrew and R. Martinez (Thomson)
- *Oxford Series Resource Books for Teachers*

Grammar books:

- *How English Works* by M. Swan and C. Waters (OUP)
- *English Grammar in Use* by R. Murphy (CUP)
- *Intermediate Language Practice* by M. Vince and P. Emmerson (Macmillan)
- *First Certificate Language Practice* by M. Vince (Macmillan)

Dictionaries:

- *Dictionary of Law* by Elizabeth A. Martin, Jonathan Law (OUP)
- *Merriam Webster's Dictionary of Law*
- *Słownik terminologii prawniczej i ekonomicznej Angielsko – Polski* J. Jaślan and H. Jaślan (Wiedza Powszechna)
- *Słownik terminologii prawniczej polsko-angielski, angielsko-polski* by E. Ożga (Oficyna Wydawnicza Branta)
- *Oxford Collocations – Dictionary for Students of English*
- *Oxford Idioms Dictionary*
- *Oxford Phrasal Verbs Dictionary*

Tests:

- *Quick Placement Test*
- *TOLES (The Test of Legal Skills)*
- *ILEC (International Legal English Certificate)*

Books:

- John Grisham's novels e.g. *The Firm, The Pelican Brief, The Client, The Rainmaker*
- The Oxford Bookworms Collection
- The Oxford Bookworms Library

Films:

- Film adaptations of John Grisham's novels e.g. *The Firm, The Pelican Brief, The Client, The Rainmaker*
- TV series: *Law and Order, Damages, Ally McBeal*

Useful links:

- Online dictionary www.ling.pl
- Online dictionary www.thefreedictionary.com/
- Online dictionary www.macmillandictionary.com/
- Free website *Learn about the Law* http://public.findlaw.com/
- Website with Legal English Resources

www.legalenglishstore.com/index.php
- TOLES website www.toles.co.uk/
- ILEC website www.legalenglishtest.org/
- Legal and Business documents www.blitz-doc.com/
- Polish Legal Acts in English
www.lexadin.nl/wlg/legis/nofr/eur/lxwepol.htm
- Access to European Union Law www.eur-lex.europa.eu/

Other teaching resources:
- a language lab equipped with a blackboard, a CD player
- a photocopier
- a DVD player
- multimedia rooms (with computers and internet access)

5. The assessment

Learners' progress in all newly learnt skills and vocabulary may be assessed by means of objective and subjective tests with the use of clear criteria that the learners are familiar with.

Receptive skills may be tested by means of the following test tasks: multiple choice, matching, paraphrasing, gap-filling or true/false etc. Test tasks for the purpose of testing speaking include guided conversations, simulations or giving short presentations.
To assess progress in written tasks such as creative writing (written assignments set by the teacher e.g. a letter of complaint, CV, report), guiding writing or sentence completion may be used.

With reference to vocabulary the following testing techniques are recommended:
- multiple choice,
- matching,
- paraphrasing,
- gap-filling true/false,
- error correction,
- translating words, expressions or sentences.

The following is a sample of short test on Constitutional Law.

5.1 Constitutional Law Test

I. Complete the gaps with the given words:

local, *Parliament*, *State*, *citizens*, *rights*, *Constitutional Tribunal*, *ministers*, *hierarchical*, *constitution (3x)*, *agreements*, *judicial*, *Court*, *president*

THE POLISH LEGAL SYSTEM

The Polish legal system is based on the continental legal system and is unified within the Polish State. There is the universally binding law and the local law. The sources of universally binding law are: the Constitution, ratified international treaties and agreements ratified by the President after the Sejm and the Senate's agreement or referenda, statutes, ratified international treaties and agreements, international treaties and agreements without ratification, regulations, decrees and the local law (binding only locally). Polish law is codified.

The 1) ________ is the supreme law. It provides the basis of the political system, guarantees the freedoms and civil 2) ________ of all Polish citizens, and determines a relationship between the legislative, executive and judicial powers, determines the highest state institutions, the organization of the government and the administration, the judiciary, territorial and administrative bodies and several of supervisory agencies. No laws may contradict the Constitution's principles and all the authorities have to comply with it. The 3) ________ ________ is the body that has a sole authority to supervise the compliance of statutory law with the 4)________, legislation, international treaties and agreements and to interpret the 5) __________.

European Union law is also considered to be the supreme law. It should be implemented into Polish internal law, if it isn't directly applied before the statutes. The other ratified international agreements have at least the same force as the statutes.

The legislative power in the Polish republic is the 6) ________ which consists of 2 chambers: the Sejm – the lower legislative body and the Senate – the upper one. The right to start a legislative process is vested in: the 7) _______ of the Cabinet, the President, a group at least 15 members of the Sejm, or 100 thousand 8)________ with a petition. Typically, the bill is voted in the Sejm then in the Senate and finally it is signed by the 9) ________. New legislation comes into force on the day of its publication in the official journal of laws called **Dziennik Ustaw** unless there is a '*vacatio legis*'.

Executive bodies issue regulations, rules and ordinances. The Council of Ministers also signs international 10) ________ which require ratification and signs the others. Regulations are issued by following authorities: The Council of Ministers (the Cabinet), the Prime Minister, The President and the National Broadcasting Council. Most regulations and rules need to be issued under statutory authority granted by the Parliament.

The 11) ________ law is issued by local administration, according to the Constitution and only on the basis given by statutes. The acts of local law are binding within the area where the issuing organ rules. There is law from **voivodeship**, but in local matters most of local governments' decisions are made by municipality's and **poviat**'s council or by the **sejmik** of the voivodeship.

The 12)________ system in Poland ensures the independence of the judiciary and consists of: the Constitutional Tribunal, the 13)________ Tribunal, as well as the Supreme14) ________, general courts (district, provincial, appeal), administrative courts, and military courts .The system of courts is 15)________. The Supreme Court has most authority.

II. WORD FORMATION Complete the chart by filling in the correct form.

Verb	Noun	Adjective/Adverb
		amended
	authority	
	constitution	
		elected
		executive

III. Complete the gaps with an appropriate preposition.

1. The Sejm shall be composed _____ 460 Deputies.
2. Elections _____ the Sejm shall be universal, equal, direct and proportional and shall be conducted _____ secret ballot.
3. The Sejm and the Senate shall be chosen each _____ a 4-year term _____ office.
4. All companies are required to conform _____ these rules.
5. Important competences are vested _____ the President of the RP
6. _____ accordance _____ the regulations you cannot enter this building.
7. She is entitled _____ the half of the property.

IV. Find the words for the definitions below.

1. to legally invalidate (v.) _ _ _ _ _ _ _
2. a right to disapprove of the process of a decision (n.) _ _ _ _
3. the state of being free from danger, damage, or worry (n.) _ _ _ _ _ _ _ _
4. acceptance or approval of what is planned or done by another (n.) _ _ _ _ _ _ _
5. former, previous (adj.) _ _ _ _ _
6. equality, as in amount, status, or character (n.) _ _ _ _ _ _
7. elector (n.) _ _ _ _ _
8. agree (v.) _ _ _ _ _ _ _
9. self-respect (n.) _ _ _ _ _ _ _
10. a draft of a law presented to a legislature to be made into law (n.) _ _ _ _

APPENDIX

A SAMPLE LESSON WITH THE USE OF AUTHENTIC MATERIALS (THE INTERNET)

Topic:	Money & Public Finances
Level:	B1/B2
Time:	2-3 teaching hours
Materials:	The template of a loan agreement http://blitz-doc.com/forms/loan_agreement.html An excerpt from the Constitution of Poland in English http://sejm.gov.pl/prawo/konst/angielski/kon1.htm

Objectives:

1. To practise speaking, reading, listening and writing.
2. To revise and introduce vocabulary on money and public finances.
3. To practise new vocabulary with the use of authentic materials

LESSON PLAN:

1. Warm up: Speaking practice MONEY PROVERBS

Students are given a list of money proverbs. They work in pairs and discuss their meanings.

MONEY PROVERBS

1. A penny saved is a penny earned.
2. Easy come, easy go.
3. Cut your coat according your cloth.
4. Lend your money and lose your friend.
5. Money has no smell.
6. Money isn't everything.
7. The best things in life are free.
8. The more you get, the more you want.

They are asked to choose the proverb they particularly agree with.

2. Practice: Integrated skills (speaking, listening, reading) A LOAN AGREEMENT

The teacher asks students questions in connection with borrowing money, for example:

1. Is there anybody you would never lend money to?
2. How often do you borrow money?
3. Have you ever taken out a bank loan?

Then students are asked to read the adapted version of the template of a loan agreement and do the tasks below:

a) Students match the halves of the sentences below, then use them to complete the template of the loan agreement.

1. The Borrower promises to pay The Lender
2. The Borrower has the right to prepay
3. The Borrower will repay
4. The Lender can then demand immediate payment of
5. The Borrower agrees to pay

a) an attorney's fee of 7% of the unpaid balance
b) the entire remaining unpaid balance of this loan
c) the whole outstanding amount at any time
d) the amount of this note in 60 equal uninterrupted monthly instalments of 1265 ZLOTYS each
e) the sum of $70,000.00

LOAN AGREEMENT

This Loan Agreement (the Agreement) is made and effective this 11th day of July, 2009,

BETWEEN: **DAH BANK** (the 'Lender'), a corporation organized and existing under the laws of the state of **POLAND** with its head office located at: **7 LIPOWA STREET IN BIAŁYSTOK, POLAND**

AND: **TEXAS LTD** (the 'Borrower'), a corporation organized and existing under the laws of the state of **POLAND** with its head office located at: **20 KOLOROWA STREET, BIAŁYSTOK, POLAND**

1. PROMISE TO PAY
Within sixty months from today, 1) ______________________________, and interest and other charges stated below.

2. RESPONSIBILITY
Although this Agreement may be signed below by more than one person, The Borrower understands that we are equally responsible as individuals for paying back the full amount.

3. BREAKDOWN OF LOAN
Amount of Loan: Other (Describe) Amount financed: Finance charge: Total of payments: Annual Rate: 8.5%

4. REPAYMENT
This is how The Borrower will repay: 2) ______________________________ on the 5TH of each month starting on the 24 August 2001, and ending on 04 August 2006.

5. PREPAYMENT
3)______________________________. If The Borrower does, or if this loan is refinanced that is, replaced by a new note, The Lender will refund the unearned finance charge, using a commonly used formula defined by the BANKING REGULATIONS for defining rebates on instalment loans

6. LATE PAYMENT FEE
Any instalment not paid within 30 days of its due date shall be subject to a late payment of 25% of the payment, not to exceed 1581 ZLOTYS for any such late instalment.

7. SECURITY
To protect The Lender, The Borrower gives what is known as a security interest or mortgage in:
THE BORROWER'S PREMISES

8. DEFAULT
If for any reason Borrower fails to make any payment on time, Borrower shall be in default. 4) ______________________________, without giving anyone further notice. If The Borrower has not paid the full amount of the loan when the final payment is due, The Lender will charge The Borrower interest on the unpaid balance at 25% per year.

9. RIGHT OF OFFSET

If this loan becomes past due, The Lender will have the right to pay this loan from any deposit or security Borrower have with The Lender without notice to The Borrower. If The Lender gives an extension of time to pay this loan, The Borrower still must repay the entire loan.

10. COLLECTION FEES

If this note is placed with an attorney for collection, then 5) ______________________________. This fee will be added to the unpaid balance of the loan.

11. CO-BORROWERS

If The Borrower is signing this Agreement as a co-borrower, The Co-Borrower agrees to be equally responsible with The Borrower for this loan.

WITNESS WHEREOF, Company and Employee have executed this Agreement as of the date first set forth above.

LENDER	BORROWER
Stephen Cochran	Bruce Jacobs
President	

b) Students read the agreement again and answer the following questions:

1. *How long is the loan agreement for?*
2. *What is the interest rate?*
3. *What happens if the borrower does not pay the instalment in 30 days?*
4. *How is the Lender secured?*
5. *When does the attorney earn the fees?*

c) Afterwards the teacher puts the students in pairs and they act out the role. One student is the lender, the other, the borrower. On the basis of the template provided above, they have to negotiate the conditions of their own loan agreement.

3. Practice: Integrated skills (speaking, listening and reading) PUBLIC FINANCES

a) The teacher writes the different names of the countries along with the currencies on the blackboard. S/he asks students to match the countries with their currencies.

1. Ukraine	a) forint
2. Lithuania	b) euro
3. Bulgaria	c) lit
4. Slovakia	d) hryvnia
5. Hungary	e) lev

Then students are asked for some more examples.

b) Students are put into groups to discuss public finances – they are provided with the statements and they are asked to give their opinions (whether they agree or disagree) and to justify their choices.

1. *The budget should be planned for a period relevant for the execution of particular tasks prescribed in it, thus not necessarily for one year only.*
2. *Stimulating the markets by increasing some public expenditure and assisting the banks threatened by bankruptcy is a better solution than decreasing public expenditure in the context of the financial crisis.*
3. *Taxes should not be raised during the financial crisis.*
4. *No reforms should be carried out during the crisis.*
5. *Poland should get accession to the euro zone as quickly as possible.*

c) Then they practice new vocabulary based on the extract from the Constitution of the Republic of Poland. They are asked to read the Constitution articles and then decide whether the sentences given below are true (T) or false (F).

THE CONSTITUTION OF THE REPUBLIC OF POLAND OF 2ND APRIL, 1997

Chapter X
PUBLIC FINANCES

Article 227

1. The central bank of the State shall be the National Bank of Poland. It shall have the exclusive right to issue money as well as to formulate and implement monetary policy. The National Bank of Poland shall be responsible for the value of Polish currency.
2. The organs of the National Bank of Poland shall be: the President of the National Bank of Poland, the Council for Monetary Policy as well as the Board of the National Bank of Poland.
3. The Sejm, on request of the President of the Republic, shall appoint the President of the National Bank of Poland for a period of 6 years.
4. The President of the National Bank of Poland shall not belong to a political party, a trade union or perform public activities incompatible with the dignity of his office.
5. The Council for Monetary Policy shall be composed of the President of the National Bank of Poland, who shall preside over it, as well as persons distinguished by their knowledge of financial matters - appointed, in equal numbers, by the President of the Republic, the Sejm and the Senate for a period of 6 years.
6. The Council for Monetary Policy shall annually formulate the aims of monetary policy and present them to the Sejm at the same time as the submission of the Council of Ministers' draft Budget. Within 5 months following the end of the fiscal year, the Council for Monetary Policy shall submit to the Sejm a report on the achievement of the purposes of monetary policy.
7. The organization and principles of activity of the National Bank of Poland, as well as detailed principles for the appointment and dismissal of its organs, shall be specified by statute.

1. The National Bank of Poland is the only institution authorised to issue money in Poland.
2. The Council for Monetary Policy is responsible for the value of Polish currency.
3. The President of the Republic of Poland is an organ of the National Bank of Poland.
4. The President of the National Bank of Poland cannot perform any public activities.
5. Members of the Council for Monetary Policy are chosen by the President of the Republic of Poland and the Parliament.

4. Homework

For homework, the teacher may ask students to draft a loan agreement they have negotiated during the class.

BIBLIOGRAPHY

Adam, S.L. & R.S. Stan, A.S. Moanga. 2011. Authentic Language Teaching Materials – Advantages and Challenges. *Bulletin UASVM Horticulture* 68: 353-356

Akbari, Z. 2011. Vocabulary comprehension and learning in an ESP context: Strategy use and knowledge sources. *The Asian ESP Journal 7:* 5-27

Alderson, J. C., Clapham, C. & D. Wall. 1995. *Language Test Construction and Evaluation.* Cambridge: Cambridge University Press.

Allen, J.P.B. 1984. General purpose language teaching: A variable focus approach. In C. J. Brumfit (Ed.). *General English Syllabus Design. ELT Documents No. 118.* London: Pergamon Press & The British Council.

Bacha, N. N. & R. Bahous. 2008. Contrasting views of business students' writing needs in an EFL environment. *English for Specific Purposes 27:* 74-93.

Bachman, L.F. & A.S. Palmer. 1996. *Language Testing in Practice.* Oxford: Oxford University Press.

Badger, R. 2003. Legal and general: towards a genre analysis of newspapers reports. *English for Specific Purposes 22*: 249-263.

Barnard, R. & D. Zemach. 2003. Materials for Special Purposes. In B. Tomlinson (Ed.). *Developing Materials for Language Teaching.* Continuum International Publishing Group.

Barron, C. 1992. Cultural Synthonicity: Co-operative Relationships Between The ESP Unit and Other Departments in *Hongkong Papers in Linguistics and Language Teaching 15.*

—. 2002. Problem-solving and EAP: themes and issues in a collaborative teaching venture *English for Specific Purposes 22*: 297-314.

Basturkmen, H. 2006. *Ideas and Options in English for Specific Purposes.* New York: Routledge.

Belcher, D. D. 2006. English for specific purposes: Teaching to perceived needs and imagined futures in worlds of work, study, and everyday life. *TESOL Quarterly*, *40(1):* 133–156.

Bell, J. & R. Gower. 1998. Writing course materials for the world: a comprise. In B. Tomlinson (Ed.). *Developing Materials for Language Teaching.* Continuum International Publishing Group.

Benavent, G.T. & S.S. Penamaria. 2011. Use of authentic materials in the ESP classroom. *Encuentro 20*:89-94.

Benesch, S. 1996. Needs Analysis and Curriculum Development in EAP: An example of a critical approach. *Teaching English to Speakers of Other Languages Quarterly*, 30 (4): 732- 738.

—. 1999. Rights Analysis: Studying power relations in an academic setting. *English for Specific Purposes* Journal *18 (4):* 313-327.

—. 2001. *Critical English for Academic Purposes: theories, politics and practice* London: Laurence Erlbaum.

Berwick, R. 1989. Needs assessment in language programming: from theory to practice. In: Johnson, R .K. (Ed). *The second language curriculum* (pp.48-62). Cambridge: Cambridge University Press.

Bhatia, V. K. 1982. *An investigation into formal and functional characteristics of qualifications in legislative writing and its application to English for academic purposes.* Unpublished doctoral dissertation, Aston University, Birmingham.

—. 1993. *Analysing Genre: Language Use in Professional Settings.* London: Longman.

—. 2002. Applied genre analysis: a multi-perspective model. *IBERICA 4*:3-19.

—. 2004. *Worlds of Written Discourse.* London: Continuum.

Bhatia, V. K. & M. Gotti.2006. *Explorations in Specialised Genres*. Bern: Peter Lang.

Black, P. Harrison, C., Lee, C., Marshall, B., & Wiliam, D. 2003. *Assessment for Learning: Putting it into Practice.* Berkshire: Open University Press.

Block, D. 1991. Some thoughts on DIY materials design. *ELT Journal 45 (3).*

Bloor, T. & Bloor, M. 1986. *Languages for Specific Purposes: Practice and theory* (occasional paper no. 19). Dublin: Trinity College.

Bocanegra-Ville, A. 2010. Evaluating and designing materials for ESP classroom. In M.F. Ruiz-Garrido, I. Fortanet-Gómez, J. C. Palmer-Silveira (Eds.) *English for Professional and Academic Purposes*. New York: Editions Rodoppi B.V.

Breen, M.P. 1984. Process in syllabus design and classroom language learning. In C. J. Brumfit (Ed.). *General English Syllabus Design. ELT Documents No. 118*. London: Pergamon Press & The British Council.

—. 1985. Authenticity in the classroom. *Applied Linguistics 6 (1):*60-70.

Breen, M.P. & C. N. Candlin 1987. Which materials? : a consumer's and designer's guide. In L.E. Sheldon (Ed.) *ELT Textbooks and Materials: Problems in Evaluation and Development. ELT Documents 126.*

Brieger, N. 2002. *Professional English LAW*. Essex: Pearson Education Limited.
Brindley, G. 1989. The role of needs analysis in adult ESL program design. In: Johnson, R .K. (Ed). *The second language curriculum* (pp.63-78). Cambridge: Cambridge University Press.
Brumfit, C.J. (Ed.). 1984. *General English Syllabus Design. ELT Documents No. 118.* London: Pergamon Press & The British Council.
Buckley, F.J. 1998. *Team Teaching: What, Why, and How?* Thousand Oaks, CA: Sage.
Canagarajah, A. S. 2005. Reconstructing local knowledge. Reconfiguring language studies. In A. S.Canagarajah (Ed.), *Reclaiming the Local in Language Policy and Practice.* Mahwah, NJ: Lawrence Erlbaum.
Candlin, C.N. 1984. Syllabus design as a critical process. In C.J. Brumfit (Ed.). *General English Syllabus Design. ELT Documents No. 118.* London: Pergamon Press & The British Council. pp. 29-46.
Candlin, C.N., V.K. Bhatia & C.H. Jensen. 2002. Developing legal writing materials for English second language learners: problems and perspective. *English for Specific Purposes 21:* 299-320.
Carter, R. 1987. Vocabulary and second / foreign language teaching. *Language Teaching, 20 (1).*
Celani, M. A. A. 2008. When myth and reality meet: Reflections on ESP in Brazil. *English for Specific Purposes 27*: 412–423.
Chambers, F. 1980. A Re-Evaluation of Needs Analysis in ESP. *The ESP Journal (1) 1:* 25-33.
Cheng, L. 2005. *Changing Language Teaching through Language Testing: a washback study*. Studies in Language Testing 21. Cambridge: Cambridge University Press.
Clapham, C. 1996. *The Development of IELTS: a study of the effect of background knowledge on reading comprehension.* Studies in Language Testing 4. Cambridge: Cambridge University Press.
Cordell, J. 2000. *Cambridge Business English Activities.* Cambridge: Cambridge University Press.
Corder, S. P. 1993. *Introducing Applied Linguistics*. London: Penguin. (Original work published in 1973).
Cowling, J.D. 2007. Needs analysis: Planning a syllabus for a series of intensive workplace courses at a leading Japanese company. *English for Specific Purposes 26* :426–442.
Coxhead, A. & Nation, P. 2001. The specialised vocabulary of English for academic purposes. In J. Flowerdew & M. Peacock (Eds.) *Research Perspectives on English for Academic Purposes* (pp.252 – 267) Cambridge: Cambridge University Press.

Crowther-Alwyn, J. 1999. *Business Roles 2.* Cambridge: Cambridge University Press.

Cunningsworth, A. 1995. *Choosing Your Coursebook.* Oxford: Heinemann.

Darian, S. 2001. Adapting authentic materials for language teaching. *English Teaching Forum:* April: 2-7.

Dastgoshadeh, A. & K. Jalizadeh. 2011. Authentic Language Materials: A new outlook. *European Journal of Scientific Research 58* (1): 84-87.

Davies, A. 2001. The logic of testing Languages for Specific Purposes. *Language Testing 18;* 133 -147.

Davies, A. 2006. What do learners really want from their EFL courses? *ELT Journal* 60 (1): 3-12.

Deutch, Y. 2003. Needs analysis for academic legal English courses in Israel: a model of setting priorities. *Journal of English for Academic Purposes 2;* 125-146.

the Directive on the Right of Citizens of the Union and their Family Members to Move and Reside Freely within the Territory of the Member States (Directive 2004/38/EC).

Donaghue, H. & H. Potten. 2000. *Clockwise Upper-intermediate.* Oxford: Oxford University Press.

Douglas, D. 2000. *Assessing Languages for Specific Purposes.* Cambridge: Cambridge University Press.

Dovey, T. 2006. What purposes, specifically? Re-thinking purposes and specificity in the context of the new vocationalism. *English for Specific Purposes 25* :387–402.

Dubin, F. & E. Olshtain. 1986. *Course Design.* Cambridge: Cambridge University Press.

Dudley-Evans, T. & M. J. St John. 1998. *Developments in English for Specific Purposes* Cambridge: Cambridge University Press.

Dumitrescu, V. 2000. Authentic materials – selection and implementation in exercise language training. *English Teaching Forum* April: 20-24.

El-Dahks, D. 2011. How to Choose your ELT Coursebook: Some Useful Guidelines. The *International Journal of the Book* 8 (1):1-10.

Elliot, J. 1999. *Action Research for Educational Change* Buckingham: Oxford University Press.

Flowerdew, J. & Peacock, M. 2001. *Research Perspectives on English for Academic Purposes* Cambridge: Cambridge University Press.

Flowerdew, L. 2005a. An integration of corpus-based and genre-based approaches to text analysis in EAP/ESP: countering criticisms against corpus-based methodologies *English for Specific Purposes* 24: 321–332.

—. 2005b. Integrating traditional and critical approaches to syllabus design: the 'what', the 'how' and the 'why? *Journal of English for Academic Purposes 4* : 135–147.
Fulcher, G. 1997. An English language placement test: issues in reliability and validity. *Language Testing 14(2):* 113-138.
—. 1999. Assessment in English for academic purposes: putting content validity in its place. *Applied Linguistics 20 (2):* 221-236.
Gaffield-Vile, N. 1996. Content-based second language instruction at the tertiary level.*ELT Journal 50 (2*):108-114.
Garrison, C., & Ehringhaus, M. 2007. *Formative and Summative Assessments in the Classroom.* Available at http://www.amle.org/Publications/WebExclusive/Assessment/tabid/1120/Default.aspx
Gatehouse, K. 2001. Key Issues in English for Specific Purposes (ESP) Curriculum Development *The Internet TESL Journal*, Vol.VII, No.10, October http://iteslj.org/Articles/Gatehouse-ESP.html
Gibbons, J. 2004. Taking Legal English seriously. In J. Gibbons, V. Prakasam, V. K. Tirumalesh, H. Nagarajan (eds.) *Language and the Law*. Hyderabad: Orient Longman Private Limited.
Gilakjani, A.P. & S.M. Ahmadi. 2011. The effect of text familiarity on Iranian EFL learners' listening comprehension. *Journal of Language Teaching and Research 2 (4):* 783-789.
Graves, K. 1996. *Teachers as course developers*. Cambridge: Cambridge University Press.
Green, A. 2007. *IELTS Washback in Context: preparation for academic writing in higher education*. Studies in Language Testing 25. Cambridge: Cambridge University Press.
Grunert, J. 1997. *The Course Syllabus: A Learner-Centered Approach*. Bolton, MA: Anker Publishing.
Guariento W. & J. Morley. 2001. Text and Task authenticity in the EFL classroom. *ELT Journal 55 (4):* 347-357.
Haigh, R. 2004. *Legal English.* New York: Cavendish Publishing Limited.
Hamp-Lyons, L. 2011. English for Academic Purposes. In Hinkel, E. 2011. *Handbook of Research in Second Language Teaching and Learning.* Vol. II. New York: Routledge.
Harding, K. 2007. *English for Specific Purposes*. Oxford: Oxford University Press.
Harmer, J. 2007. *The Practice of English Language Teaching.* Harlow: Pearson Education Limited.
Henning, G. 1987. *A Guide to Language Testing.* Cambridge, Mass: Newbury House.

Hutchinson, T. & A. Waters. 1987. *English for Specific Purposes: A Learning-centred approach*. Cambridge: Cambridge University Press.
Hyland, K. 2002. Specificity revisited: how far should we go now? *English for Specific Purposes* 21:385–395.
Hyland,K. & L. Hamp-Lyons. 2002. EAP: issues and directions. *Journal of English for Academic Purposes, 1:*1-12.
ILEC Handbook for teachers. 2006. University of Cambridge ESOL Examinations
Ingels, M. B. 2006. *Legal English Communication Skills*. Lueven: Acco.
Islam, C. & Mares, C. 2003. Adapting classroom materials. In B. Tomlinson (Ed.). *Developing Materials for Language Teaching*. London: Continuum International Publishing Group.
Iwai, T., Kondo, K., Limm, S. J. D., Ray, E. G., Shimizu, H., and Brown, J. D. 1999. *Japanese Language Needs Analysis*. Available at: http://www.nflrc.hawaii.edu/Networks/NW13/NW13.pdf
Jackson, J. 1998. Reality based decisions cases in ESP teacher education: Windows on Practice. *English for Specific Purposes (2):* 151-167.
Jensen, C. & Hansen, C. 1995. The effect of prior knowledge on EAP listening-test performance. *Language Testing 12*, 99-119.
Jeong, Ch. 2005. Learner Needs Analysis for T&I Program Reform. *Meta: Translator Journal*, vol.5, no 4.
Johns, A.M. 2004. *Defining and Teaching Genre*. TESOL Conference, March 31, 2004.
Jopek-Bosiacka, A. 2008. *Przekład Prawny i Sądowy*. Warszawa: Wydawnictwo Naukowe PWN.
Jordan, R. 1997. *English for Academic Purposes* Cambridge: Cambridge University Press.
Kemmis, S. & McTagart, R. 2000. Participatory Action Research: Communicative Action and the Public Sphere" in: Denzin, N.K., Lincoln, Y.S (eds.): *the Sage Handbook of Qualitative Research* 559-604.
Kim, S. 2006. Academic oral communication needs of East Asian international graduate students in non-science and non-engineering fields. *English for Specific Purposes* 25: 479–489.
Komorowska, H. 2002. *Sprawdzanie umiejętności w nauce języka obcego. Kontrola – Ocena – Testowanie*. Warszawa: Fraszka Edukacyjna
—. 2006. *Programy nauczania w kształceniu ogólnym i kształceniu językowym* Warszawa: Fraszka Edukacyjna.
Koshy, V. 2005. *Action Research for Improving Practice* London: Sage Publications, Inc.

—. 2009. *Action Research for Improving Educational Practice. A Step-By-Step Guide* London: Sage Publications, Inc.
Krashen, S.D. 1982. *Principles and Practice in Second Language Acquisition*. Oxford: Pergamon.
Krekeler, C. 2006. Language for special academic purposes (LSAP) testing: the effect of background knowledge revisited. *Language Testing 23:* 99-130.
Krois-Lindner, A. & Translegal. 2006. *International Legal English. Cambridge:* Cambridge University Press.
Lee, W. Y. 1995. Authenticity revisited: text authenticity and learner authenticity *ELT Journal 49 (4):* 323-328.
Lewkowicz, J.A. 2000. Authenticity in language testing: some outstanding questions. *Language Testing 17*: 43-64.
Lockwood, J.2012. Developing an English for specific purpose curriculum for Asian call centres: How theory can inform practice. *English for Specific Purposes* 31: 14–24.
Long, M.H. 1996. The role of the linguistic environment in the second language acquisition. In W.C. Richie & T.K. Bhatia (Eds.) *Handbook of second language acquisition* (pp.413-468). San Diego: Academic Press.
Long, M.H. & Crookes, G. 1992. Three approaches to task-based syllabus design. *TESOL Quarterly, 26(1)*, 27-55.
Mackay, R. & A. Mountford.1978. *English for Specific Purposes: a case study approach*. London: Longman.
MacDonald, M., Badger, R. & G. White. 2000. The real thing?: authenticity and academic listening. *English for Specific Purposes 19*: 253-267.
Mason, C. & R. Atkins. 2007. *The Lawyer's English Coursebook.* Stamford: Global Legal English Ltd.
Matejka, K. & L. B. Kurke. 1994. Designing a Great Syllabus. *College Teaching 42*: 115-117.
McDonough, J. 1984. *ESP in perspective: a practical guide.* London: Collins ELT.
McDonough, J. & C. Shaw. 1993. *Materials and Methods in ELT: a teacher's guide*. Oxford: Blackwell Publishing.
McGrath, I. 2002. *Materials Evaluation and Design for Language Teaching*. Edinburgh: Edinburgh University Press.
McNamara, T.F. 2000. *Language Testing.* Oxford: Oxford University Press.
McNamara, T.F. & C. Roever. 2006. *Language Testing: the social dimension.* Oxford: Blackwell Publishing.

Mertel, C.A. 2006. *Action Research Teachers as Researchers in the Classroom* London: Sage Publications, Inc.
Mishan, F. 2005. *Designing Authenticity into Language Learning. Materials*. Bristol: Intellect Books.
Misztal, M. 1994. *Tests in English. Thematic Vocabulary*. Warszawa: Wydawnictwa Szkolne i Pedagogiczne.
Morrow, K. 1977. Authentic Texts in ESP. In S. Holden (Ed.), *English for Specific Purposes*. London: Modern English Publications.
Munby, J.1978. *Communicative Syllabus Design*. Cambridge: Cambridge University Press.
Mukundan, J. & T. Ahour. 2010. A review of textbook evaluation. Checklists across four decade (1970-2008). In B. Tomlinson & H. Masuhara (Eds.). *Research for Materials Development in Language Learning: Evidence for Best Practice*. London: Continuum International Publishing Group.
Nation, I. S. P. 1990. *Teaching and Learning Vocabulary*. New York: Newbury House/Harper-Collins.
Nation, P. 2001. *Learning Vocabulary in Another Language*. Cambridge: Cambridge University Press.
—. 2003. Materials for Teaching Vocabulary. In B. Tomlinson (Ed.) *Developing Materials for Language Teaching*. London: Continuum.
Nelson, M. 2000. A corpus-based study of Business English and Business English teaching materials. University of Manchester available at: http://users.utu.fi/micnel/business_english_lexis_site.htm
Northcott, J. & G. Brown. 2006. Legal translator training: Partnership between teachers of English for legal purposes and legal specialists. *English for Specific Purposes 25:* 358–375.
Nunan, D. 1988. *Syllabus Design*. Oxford: Oxford University Press.
—. 1989. *Designing Tasks for the Communicative Classroom*. Cambridge: Cambridge University Press.
Oxenden, C. & Ch. Latham – Koenig. 2001. *English File Upper-intermediate*. Oxford: Oxford University Press.
Pahl, N. & A. Richter. 2007. *SWOT Analysis – Idea, Methodology and a Practical Approach. Scholarly Research Paper*. Norderstedt: GRIN Verlag.
Paltridge, B. 2006. *Discourse Analysis: an introduction*. London: Continuum.
Parkes, J. & Harris, M. 2002. The purposes of a syllabus. *College Teaching 50 (2):* 55-61.
Peacock, M. 1997. The effect of authentic materials on the motivation of EFL learners. *ELT Journal 51 (2):* 144-156 Oxford University Press.

Pennycook, A. 1997. Vulgar pragmatism, critical pragmatism, and EAP. *English for Specific Purposes, 16 (4)* : 253-269.
Peretz, A.S. & Shoham, M. 1990. Testing reading comprehension in LSP: does topic familiarity affect assessed difficulty and actual performance? *Reading in a Foreign Language* 7: 447-455.
Pieńkos, J. 1999. *Podstawy Juryslingwistyki: Język w prawie – Prawo w języku*. Warszawa: Oficyna Prawnicza. MUZA SA.
Prabhu, N.S. 1984. Procedural syllabuses. In T.E. Read (Ed.). *Trends in Language Syllabus Design.* Singapore: Singapore University Press/RELC. 272-280.
Rabbani, G. 2006. Syllabus vs. Curriculum. *Meet the Horizon.* Available at:http://www.essaydepot.com/essayme/4145/index.php
Rea-Dickins, P. & K. Germaine. 1992. *Evaluation.* Oxford: Oxford University Press.
Read, J. 1990. Providing relevant content in an EAP writing test. *English for Specific Purposes 9*: 109-121.
Robinson, P. 1991. *ESP Today: a Practitioner's Guide.* Hemel Hempstead: Prentice Hall International.
Rubdy, R. 2003. Selection of Materials. In B. Tomlinson (Ed.). *Developing Materials for Language Teaching.* London: Continuum International Publishing Group.
Sagor, R. 2007. *Action Research Guidebook* London: Sage Publications, Inc.
Saraceni, C. 2003. Adapting courses: a critical view. In B. Tomlinson (Ed.). *Developing Materials for Language Teaching.* London: Continuum International Publishing Group.
Schane, S. A. 2006. *Language and the Law.* London: Continuum.
Schmuck, A. 2008. *Practical Action Research: A Collection of Articles* London: Corwin Press
Sener, J. 2007. In search of student-generated content in online education. *E-mentor* No 4 (27) available at http://www.e-mentor.edu.pl/_xml/wydania/21/467.pdf
Ses˅ek, U. 2007. English for teachers of EFL – Toward a holistic description. *English for Specific Purposes 26*: 411-425.
Sheldon, L.E. 1988. Evaluating ELT textbooks and materials. *ELT Journal, 42* (4).
Shohamy, E. 2001. *The Power of Tests: a critical perspective on the uses of language tests.* Harlow: Pearson Education Limited.
Shomoossi, N. & S. Ketabi. 2007. A critical look at the concept of authenticity. *Electronic Journal of Foreign Language Teaching 4 (1):*149-155.

Sierocka, H. 2011. *Legal English – Niezbędnik przyszłego prawnika.* Białystok: Publikator.

Sifakis, N.C. 2003. Applying the adult education framework to ESP curriculum development: an integrative model. *English for Specific Purposes 25:* 195-211.

Sinclair, J.M. & A. Renouf. 1988. A lexical syllabus for language learning. In R. Carter and M. McCarthy (Eds.) *Vocabulary and Language Teaching*. London: Longman.

Smith, T. 2000. *Business Law.* London: Longman.

Songhori, M.H. 2008. Introduction to Needs Analysis. *English for Specific Purposes World* 4: 1-25.

Spector-Cohen, E. Kirschner, M., & C. Wexler, C. 2001. Designing EAP reading courses at the university level. *English for Specific Purposes,* 20: 367-386.

Spratt, M. 1999. How good are we at knowing what learners like. *System* 27 : 141-155.

Stern, H.H. 1984. Introduction, review and discussion. In C. J. Brumfit (ed.) 1984 *General English Syllabus Design. ELT Documents No. 118.* London: Pergamon Press & The British Council.

Strevens, P. 1988. ESP after twenty years: a re-appraisal. In M. Tickoo (Ed.) *ESP: State of the Art.* Singapore: SEAMEO Regional Language Centre.

Stufflebeam, D.L. & Shinkfield, A.J. 2007. *Evaluation theory models and applications.* San Francisco: Jossey-Bass.

Swales, J. 1981. Aspects of articles introductions. *University of Aston ESP Research Reports,* No. 1.

—. 1990. *Genre Analysis.* Cambridge: Cambridge University Press.

Taillefer, G.F. 2007. The professional language needs of Economics graduates: Assessment and perspectives in the French context. *English for Specific Purposes* 26, 26:135-155.

Taylor, D. 1994. Inauthentic Authenticity or Authentic Inauthenticity? *TESL-EJ* Vol.1, No2 A-1 available at http://www.cc.kyoto-su.ac.jp/information/tesl-ej/ej02/a.1.html 08.07.2007

Thomas, B.J. 1995. *Advanced Vocabulary & Idiom.* Essex: Longman Group Limited.

Tomlinson, B. 2001. Materials development. In Carter, R, and D. Nunan. (eds.) *The Cambridge Guide to Teaching English to Speakers of Other Language.* Cambridge: Cambridge University Press.

—. 2003. Materials evaluation. In B. Tomlinson (Ed.). *Developing Materials for Language Teaching.* London: Continuum International Publishing Group.

—. 2012. State-of-the Art Article. Materials development for language learning and teaching. *Language Teaching 45.2:*143-179.

Tomlinson, B. & H. Masuhara. 2003. Simulations in materials development. In B. Tomlinson (Ed.). *Developing Materials for Language Teaching.* London: Continuum International Publishing Group.

Tratnik, A. 2008. Key issues in testing English for Specific Purposes. *Scripta Manent 4* (1) 3-13.

Tsao, C. 2011. English for Specific Purposes in the EFL Context: A survey of student and faculty perceptions. *The Asian ESP Journal Volume 7*: 126-149.

Tyler, R.W., Madaus, G.F.& D.L. Stufflebeam. 1989. *Educational Evaluation: Classic Works of Ralph W. Tyler.* Boston: Kluwier Academic Publishers.

Tyler, R.W. 1949. *Basic Principles of Curriculum and Instruction.* Chicago: The University of Chicago Press.

Vaiciuniene, V. & D. Uzpaliene. 2010. Authentic resources in technology based ESP learning. *Studies about Languages* 17: 94:98.

van der Walt, J.L. & F. Steyn (Jr.). 2008. The validation of language tests. *Stellenbosch Papers in Linguistics 38*: 191-204.

Wagner, A. 2003.Translation of the language of the common law into Legal French: Myth or Reality. *International Journal for the Semiotics of Law 16:* 177-193.

Wallwork, A. 1997. *Discussions A-Z. Intermediate.* Cambridge: Cambridge University Press.

Watson Todd, R. 2003. EAP or TEAP? *Journal of English for Academic Purposes*, 2(2) 61-70.

Weigle, S. C. 2002. *Assessing Writing*. Cambridge: Cambridge University Press.

West, R. 1994. Needs analysis in language teaching. *Language Teaching, 27/1*: 1-19.

West, R. 1998. *ESP- State of the art.* Available at: www.man.ac.uk/CELSE/esp/west.htm

Wharton, S. 1999. *From postgraduate student to publisher writer: Discourse variation and development in TESOL.* Unpublished doctoral dissertation, Aston University, Birmingham.

White, R. 1988. *The ELT Curriculum.* Oxford: Blackwell Publishing.

Wholey, J.S., Hatry, H.P. & K.E. Newcomer (eds.). 2010. *Handbook of Practical Program Evaluation.* San Francisco: Jossey-Bass.

Widdowson, H. G. 1978. *Teaching Language as Communication*. Oxford: Oxford University Press.

—. 1979. *Explorations in Applied Linguistics*. Oxford: Oxford University Press.
—. 1983. *Learning Purpose and Learning Use*. Oxford: Oxford University Press.
—. 1984. Educational and pedagogic factors in syllabus design in C.J. Brumfit (ed.) *General English Syllabus Design. ELT Documents No. 118*. London: Pergamon Press & The British Council.
—. 1994. The Ownership of English. *TESOL Quarterly 28:* 377-389.
—. 1998. Communication and Community: The Pragmatics of ESP. *English for Specific Purposes*, *1*:1-13.
—. 2003. *Defining Issues in English Language Teaching* Oxford: Oxford University Press.
Wilkins, D. 1976. *Notional Syllabuses.* Oxford: Oxford University Press.
Wong, V., Kwok, P. & N. Choi. 1995. The use of authentic materials at tertiary level. *ELT Journal* 49/4: 318-322.
Woznak, S. 2010. Language needs analysis from a perspective of international professional mobility: The case of French mountain guides. *English for Specific Purposes 29*: 243-252.
Wu, H. & R.G. Badger. 2009. In a strange and uncharted land: ESP teachers' strategies for dealing with unpredicted problems in subject knowledge during class. *English for Specific Purposes, 28*: 19-32.
Wu, W.M. & C.W. Stansfield. 2001. Towards authenticity of task in test development. *Language Testing 18*: 187:206.
Yalden, J. 1984. Syllabus design in general education. In C. J. Brumfit (ed.) 1984 *General English Syllabus Design. ELT Documents No. 118.* London: Pergamon Press & The British Council. 29-46.
Zhang, Z. 2007. Towards an integrated approach to teaching Business English: A Chinese experience. *English for Specific Purposes,* 26: 399-410.

Dictionaries

Dictionary of Language Testing. 1999. A. Davies (ed.) Cambridge University Press
Dictionary of Law (OUP)
Merriam Webster's Dictionary of Law
Online dictionary www.ling.pl
Online dictionary www.thefreedictionary.com/
Oxford Collocations – Dictionary for Students of English
Słownik terminologii prawniczej i ekonomicznej Angielsko – Polski by J. Jaślan and H. Jaślan (Wiedza Powszechna)

Routledge Encyclopedia of Language Teaching and Learning. 2004. M. Byram. (ed.)

Links

http://www.britishcouncil.org/pl/poland-legal-english.htm
http://toles.tricycle-media.com/exec/sam/view/id=195/node=198/

INDEX